# 7 STEPS TO PSYCHIC MIND CONTROL

Copyright © 1980 by Maximum Exposure Advertising, Inc.

All rights reserved. No part of this book may be reproduced or utilized in any form or by any means, electronic or mechanical, including photocopying, recording or by any information storage and retrieval system, without permission in writing from the Publisher. Inquiries should be addressed to Maximum Exposure Advertising, Inc., 801 Second Avenue, Suite 705, New York, N.Y. 10017.

Printed in the United States of America.

# CONTENTS

| | | |
|---|---|---|
| ABOUT THE AUTHORS | | 9 |
| PREFACE | | 11 |
| INTRODUCTION | | 13 |

    What The Hell Is This All About?
    How Do We Do It?
    This Sounds Freaky. I Don't Get It.
    How Fast Does It Work?
    Why Isn't HRF In Use On A Mass Level?
    What If The Women Find Out?

I  **Step One: DO I LIKE ME?**    21
    What Causes Inferiority?
    What Is Integrity?
    The Pavlov Method

II  **Step Two: PEACE = PIECE**    31
    How Do I Get Peace?
    How Do I Clean My Mind?
    What Kind Of Peaceful Thoughts Should
      I Think About?
    When's The Best Time For TM?

III  **Step Three: MAY THE FORCE BE WITH YOU**    39
    What Is The Secret To Interest?
    How Not To Be Boring
    What's My *Body* Doing All This Time?

IV  **Step Four: WHY NOT THE BEST?**    51
    The Mack The Knife Factor
    How Can I Be Like Machiavelli?

Changing Partners: How Machiavellian
  Thinking Can Help You Dump A Broad
What If She Dumps *Me?*
How Can I Fuck Her Mind?
Machiavellian Group Therapy

## V Step Five: DON'T THINK OF DEFEAT— THINK OF DE BROAD     61
What Are My *Wildest* Dreams?
What If I *Can't* Fantasize?
If You Can Get Into It Mentally, You Can
  Get Into It Physically (Or Literally)
Physical Defects
Physical And Mental Domination
Marriage To A JAP
Can JAPs Be Cured?
The Name Game

## VI Step Six: WILL SHE THINK I'M A CREEP: THE TM FACTOR     75
How To Avoid Worry
What Happens When The Mind Is Empty?
Benefits of TM: How To Talk To Women
Clichés
What Next?
Benefits of TM: Silence Is Golden
Listening
Summing Up Listening
Outward Appearances: What Should I Wear?
TM: One Final Point

## VII Step Seven: GOD IS MY CO-PILOT     87
God As A Partner
Does God Want Me To Be A Stud?

### RABID RESULTS     93
Guys…
… And Dolls

> "*The ability to entertain to get a message across is retained in the brain far longer than a barrage of cold textbook information.*"
>
> —Peter Cushey, Star and House Surgeon of Hammy Film Studios, on the occasion of the studio's being knighted by the Queen in London—April, 1968

## "7 STEPS TO PSYCHIC MIND CONTROL"
## Disclaimer Claimer

For illustrative purposes, we have created some specious researchers and doctors whose experiments, although fictitious, have served to exemplify the totally *valid* conclusions set forth in this book. We genuinely feel that this pseudo-scientific approach to the serious business of psychic mind control acutely defines the theories and properties behind the seven steps. We further feel that the data, so thoroughly discussed in the following chapters, will be of immense aid in improving one's more-than-likely decrepit romantic lifestyle.

# ABOUT THE AUTHORS

Doctors X, Y, and Z felt it necessary to briefly discuss their backgrounds, as they reasoned a normally sexually inhibited person wouldn't be at ease with just any average group of quacks.

## DOCTOR X

Doctor X was and is one of the country's foremost authorities on bladders and anal cavities. His renowned work, *The Amazing Mr. Penis*, a layman's look at urinalysis, sold out in a record-breaking two weeks—truly a feat for a tome of this sort.

Sex organ consultant to the stars, Dr. X is currently working on his second book, an in-depth study of Brian Eno.

Always looking ahead for new and interesting approaches to medicine, Dr. X is presently working night and day on the concept of synthetic flesh.

## DOCTOR Y

If Sigmund Freud wasn't dead, he would be mighty proud of Dr. Y. When it comes to sex drives, nobody works harder and twice as long as this man. Holder of every degree possible in the world of psychiatry, Dr. Y, were his name made public, would probably become one of the libido legends of the twentieth century. He wishes, however, to remain anonymous—thereby giving him the freedom to co-write books such as this one; in short, to devote himself unselfishly to those who require mental help, or, as he says, "to help balance the unbalanced."

Always breaking new ground, Dr. Y was the first one to champion Veterinary Psychiatry. His treatise on this subject, "The Jung Lions," became the rage of Vienna in 1963. This is just par for the course for the doctor whose only desire is to " ... boldly go where no man has gone before."

More recently, Dr. Y's unorthodox essays have appeared in such influential periodicals as *Psychology Today, Family Health*, and *Film Comment*.

## DOCTOR Z

The third prong in our scientific triangle belongs to this man of theology and infinite wisdom. He provides the spiritual or psychic element in relation to the physical and mental factors—so important in a study such as this one.

Several years ago, Dr. Z made gospel history when, while trying to account for three missing days in his life, he underwent hypnosis (his first meeting with Dr. Y). Once in a trance, the doctor recounted a fabulous tale about being abducted aboard a UFO. Listening to the tapes made afterwards, Dr. Z, already an accomplished minister, became ecstatic with joy and spread the message, in a series of now-famous sermons, of how he had touched God. This incident, along with his expertise at Bingo, has made him instantly recognizable in religious circles the world over.

Prior to his collaboration on this book, Dr. Z was personal consultant to such eminent holy figures as the late Bishop Sheen, Cardinal Cooke, and Danny Thomas.

# PREFACE

X, Y, and Z, while all Americans, first met several years ago in the dissecting lab at the University of Klaussenburg.

Each was involved in his own separate work: X was studying medicine under Colin Clive; Y, whose speciality was psychiatry, was a student of Dr. Theo van Helsing; and Z, a theologist, was a protégé of Father Sandor.

Comparing notes, the three discovered that their individual research was all too obviously leading them in similar directions. They decided to join forces and embark on a collaborative project.

# INTRODUCTION

*"What The Hell Is This All About?"*

This is probably the question you are asking yourselves right now. Well, that seems fair. After all, you spent hard-earned dollars on this book. You deserve an answer.

The purpose of our project was to study the physical, mental, and spiritual habits of our soldiers, state officials, and law enforcement agents. This led to many interesting conflicts and observations, as well as a few laughs.

The end result of this survey was the amazing discovery that once the three of us combined our respective fields, we could cure virtually *any* problem affecting our country's leaders—problems which, we might add, if not remedied, could cause, in a moment of foolishness, the destruction of our entire planet!

*How Do We Do It?*

This is another good question. The answer is that by using the mind and the body in conjunction with one another, one may call upon the Higher Power. What is the Higher Power? Basically, it is the total control of one's self. That's right. Mastering the Higher Power is learning to use one's self. However, like a musical instrument, one must learn to play correctly, and, to develop a technique before one goes out into the world for a public (or private) demonstration. Not that we are saying that this book will enable you to play with yourself. You probably have already done this. In all probability, the reason you have bought this book is to learn to play with other people—preferably (but not necessarily) with women. If anything, this book will demonstrate how to "use" *yourself*—in short, to call forth the inbred powers within you (that's right—everybody's got 'em!)—and get *results*!

*This Sounds Freaky. I Don't Get It.*

You're not supposed to *get* it—you're supposed to *do* it —and believe us, it's not as difficult or "freaky" as it sounds.

Now for years there have been books about self-help— which you probably have been laughing at. Well, you shouldn't have. They had some very valid things to say. The fact is, however, that they missed the boat entirely on the reaons *why* one should attempt to find "true happiness"—some of these volumes don't even give reasons for becoming—for want of a better word— "happy". Others gave the *wrong* reason. The end result: millions of chuckling idiots romping around the world not knowing why they feel so good. You see, just "feeling good" is not enough. One must have motivation; the individual is given a greater sense of accomplishment once he knows *why* he is happy, and, that he alone has conquered a *specific* problem.

Now here's where we get down to brass tacks. When we were working on our research project we discovered, after comparing extensive notes, that *all* problems— physical, mental, and spiritual—merely boiled down to two things: MONEY and SEX—and not in that order.

Well, we reasoned, high-ranking government officials obviously aren't the only ones suffering from this ailment; there must be millions of greedy, horny people in our country alone, to say nothing of the entire world. In one bold move we discreetly "cut out", taking our valuable notes with us. We dropped our names and took on letters as monikers, the reason for this being that the government would be very upset if they knew their sex lives were leaking out—no pun intended.

After conducting a thorough investigation throughout the country, we decided that our system, broken down into 7 steps, was ready for publication. (See Chapter 9 of this book and judge our results via actual quotes and interviews from several of our many happy recipients.) If this book takes off, we plan to open our own institute. (Unfortunately, it may have to be outside of the U.S.)

*How Fast Does It Work?*

Quite simply, it works as fast as you do. Once the 7 steps have been mastered, five minutes is the maximum it should take to exert the power over those whom you wish to dominate.

You see, once we can awaken your subconscious and call upon that higher power, there literally is *no* holding you back. This innate desire—born in *everyone*—for success in the areas of money and sex have convinced us to combine our seven steps into one simple, easily memorized term: HRF—or, the Harold Robbins Factor. Again, everyone has this within them *somewhere* and whether your particular hangup is sex or money or both, HRF will enable you to pursue these desires and, most importantly, to succeed!

*Why Isn't HRF In Use On A Mass Level?*

It will be. Give us time. Although no one, to our knowledge, has really written about applying these forces for this particular purpose, the actual powers themselves are as old as all Creation. Indeed, as we have mentioned before, man has been aware of this inborn gift of achievement and has used it in the past to acquire many things. (As to what these many things are, we suggest that you go to the self-help department of any bookstore. We're not here to spiel Peale; we're pushing XYZ!)

What we are basically saying is that we only discovered a different approach to HRF—we did not invent it. Yet, throughout history, there have been a few men clever enough to apply these powers correctly—one in particular: that supreme user of HRF, the greatest teacher who ever lived and who still lives. At this point, there can be no doubt in your minds of whom we are speaking—Hugh Hefner! Hef has built up an incredible empire based entirely on money and sex. Sure, he used his uncanny knack for business, but that's exactly what we're talking about. He's worth millions a year. Beautiful women beg him to be allowed to expose themselves in his magazines and clubs. What gives someone that "uncanny" ability? Can *he* explain it. We doubt it. But whether Hef knows it or not, he's used his HRF to the fullest power—and if he can do it, you can do it!

*What If The Women Find Out?*

The minute you try some moves using your new self—they'll know it anyway. They'll feel it. What's more, they'll desire it—and, most importantly, they'll love you all the more for having mastered it.

Now let us explain this. Women are different from men. (You may have already heard a rumor to this effect—although ... Well, take our word for it—it's true.) Now, we're not just saying "physically"; why, every Hell's Angel knows *that*! No sir, we're talking about spiritually. A woman's mystery is due, in part, to an almost total reversal of HRF. You see, they know they have some kind of power over men. Their problem is not knowing *how* to use it, but *when* to use it. This makes the difference between a dynamite chick (New York City, Hollywood, Paris, Studio 54) and a cock teaser (Glendale, California).

It is partially because of this that in today's emergence of women as equals, the ladies find themselves faced with many problems—but don't let this would-be insecure susceptibility fool you. A chick can look at a guy just once and, more often than not, have him pegged—just like that! A man can be with a woman all of his life, love her, care for her, live for her—and *still* never entirely *know* her. This is the edge that all females have on us. This is power, and it is a power with which all women are endowed. They probably got it way back in the Garden of Eden when God most likely reasoned: "OK, you can have sex, but you stand the chance of being knocked up. On top of that, when you drop the kid you'll have pain." To make up for what might have started out as just a fun night on the town, God gave the women something in return. Now, it's not that he gave them *different* powers than he gave men—he just made them *aware* of these powers; unfortunately, if you saw *Oh, God*, you'll know that He can be a sly little fellow. So, although women were made aware of their powers, they really weren't made *totally* aware. Of course, this could have all been part of the Lord's Divine Plan to create analysis, but we doubt it. If anything, this silly parable has merely illustrated what we alluded to earlier: that women are spiritually, as well as physically, different from men.

Imagine, then, what women will be like once you have gained control of your own powers. You'll be that much closer to them, a fact they'll immediately recognize, appreciate ... and envy.

While there's no law, of course, forbidding women to buy this book and master control over their already overt powers (several women *have* used this book; you'll meet some of them in the last chapter), this study is primarily for men. We are not being chauvinistic. Au contraire. In order for men to make female conquests, they must understand women, and to understand women is to accept them as equals. HRF is the ultimate equalizer.

(One more thing. Although HRF can certainly be used to help you make bucks, we will concentrate on its abilities to help you make broads, which we discovered to be the far more important of the basic two problems plaguing the vast numbers of our male populace.)

*How Do I Start?*

You start by realizing that HRF is mainly a device to help you gain self-confidence. Look in the mirror and ask yourself, "Would I buy a used car from this man?" If the answer is "no", then you've got problems. Solving these problems is the name of the game. To do this there are several factors involved. For example, working hard *is* important—but not important enough to drive you to an early grave, even if you do go Fugazy. The hard (and only) fact is that there's only *one* thing that matters in this world—that's *you*—and it's high time you knew it!

First, you must learn that in order to be a success with women, you have to be a success with *you*! Remember, no woman can be dominated unless she wants to be dominated. Domination hinges a great deal on respect. For her to respect you, you must respect yourself. HRF breeds self-confidence and self-confidence reeks of respect. After all, if you don't care, why should she?

More important, in order to have success, you have to want it—and in order to want it, you have to enjoy it! Memorize the following four rules:

1. I like to have fun.
2. I want to be like Machiavelli—whoever the hell he was (is).
3. I look out for *me*, first and always, and, as most of you have already discovered, especially when it comes to women:
4. Honesty is not necessarily the best policy

Bearing this in mind, you are now ready to attempt to master the "Seven Steps to Psychic Mind Control." OK students—turn the page and prepare to know thyself ...

**GO NO FURTHER...** unless you truly believe and wish to learn the principles of HRF. **IF YOU DO NOT BELIEVE,** return to page 11 and reread all information through page 18. Keep rereading it until the text at last begins to permeate your unreasonable, stubborn, irrational, inferiority-strewn, and biased mind.

# Step One: DO I LIKE ME?

# I

If you asked yourself out for a date, would you go? What's that? You have to do your hair tonight?

If you don't go out with women, don't have many friends, or don't even like to do things by yourself, obviously you do not like *you*. Somewhere along the line you must have gotten a rejection, probably from a female. OK, so ask yourself: *Why* am I a jerk with women? Nine times out of ten—oh, hell—*ten* times out of ten, the answer is: Because you think you're inferior. Naturally, if you have no self-confidence—if you don't believe in you—you reason that the foxy redhead in your office will think you're a schmoe. Is it the way you look? Are you short and pudgy? Do you wear glasses? Do you talk funny? If the answer to all these questions is "yes", don't worry ... in fact, congratulations! You've just admitted that you're Henry Kissinger, and we all know how well he does with women!

Before his marriage, Dr. K's adventures singularly kept the National Enquirer in the black. His liaisons with beautiful women are known the world over. Obviously, if outward appearance played a major factor, the former Secretary of State would be sitting alongside you tonight in his underwear watching that by-now-unbearable rerun of "The Odd Couple" and eating lukewarm frozen lasagne. No, outward appearance is not as important as you might think. It is your appearance on the *inside* that has to be refurbished and this brings us back to the term "self-confidence." (Step 6, Chapter 7, will deal more thoroughly with the importance placed on appearance.)

However, at this point, you're probably so fucked up anyway that you place little credence in what we say. Therefore, we will illustrate with an example. We were lecturing on HRF at the bowling alley in Netcong, New Jersey one night when a shriveled little man entered. We were surprised to discover later that he was only 25 years of age. "Excuse me," he said, "but could you see me after your lecture? I have a problem." Never turning down a man in need, we readily agreed and arranged to meet him in our bungalow directly after the Bingo game. One hour passed, then two. It looked like he wasn't going to show. Finally, as Dr. Y prepared to embark for town (to see what had happened to the pizza we had ordered), he spied a pathetic little figure sitting on our steps. You guessed it. It was the little man. "What are you doing down there," Dr. Y asked.

"Oh, I've been here for hours."

"Why didn't you come in?"

"I didn't wish to disturb you. It seemed so quiet."

We all looked at each other. If anyone needs self-confidence, it's this clown, we reasoned. We asked him in and sat him down on our bed.

"Now tell us what you think is wrong."

"I have a problem," the little man said.

"Yes?"

"I desire women."

Well, that was no problem.

"I never get them."

That was.

"What do you do for a living?"

"I'm a traveling salesman."

"Well," we said, "we can't have you ruining the debauched reputation of that degenerate profession, can we?"

The little man smiled. It was the first time he had attempted any form of "happiness." He wasn't good at it.

"Well, it's like tonight. I went into this bar and asked this woman if she wanted a drink. She turned to me, laughed, and said that I looked like a frog."

"What did you do?"

"I left."

"Tell me something," asked Dr. Y, "bar-hopping aside, do you like to hop around other places—streets, meadows, ponds?"

"No."

"Do you eat flies?" asked Dr. X.

"No."

"Are you of French heritage?"

"No!" The little man was getting noticeably upset.

"Then you're not a frog!" we all chimed.

"Well thanks a lot!"

"We just wanted *you* to know it."

"That's terrific. I'm no Burt Reynolds either."

This was true. As outward appearances go, this poor specimen certainly was no Burt Reynolds. In fact, the lady in question, the one in the bar, obviously had an astute sense of character judgement; as the little man actually *did* look like a frog, a point we decided to wisely refrain from stating.

"There is one way I *am* like a frog. I'm green—with women!"

"Say, that was a clever analogy," said Dr. Z. "You obviously have wit. Do these young women know this?"

"*I* don't even know it!" he cried, scratching his head.

"Well you should!" replied Z, who wrote out something on a small index card. He then handed the man the card. On the card was written the following: "I can do all the things that Burt Reynolds can do. I have the same equipment—it's just arranged differently."

"What'll I do with this?" asked the perplexed, poor soul.

"Read it aloud three times each morning after you get up and each night before you retire," Z advised.

Y added, "Why don't you try it now?"

The little man did. He smiled—a different smile from the one he had first attempted. He seemed to glow. Although there was a long way to go, we had definitely started something.

Subsequently, we have heard from this "frog" man. He has become one of the top salesmen in his company. No more Netcong, N.J. His territory now covers Los Angeles, Hollywood, and San Francisco. As for the problem with women, he assures us that the towns through which his business takes him now abound in illegitimate little tadpoles. Once again, this is just an example of what self-confidence, or a good inward appearance, can do.

## *What Causes Inferiority?*

An inferiority complex can be caused by many things. Psychiatrists *love* to play around with this one. Usually, an inferiority complex goes back to one's childhood. In school, for example, were your *brothers* and *sisters* always getting higher marks than you? If you had no brothers and sisters, were your *friends* doing better scholastically? If you had no friends, were your *parents* always going on about what great students they used to be? You *did* have parents, didn't you! Well, it doesn't matter—because we've never heard of your brothers and sisters, your friends, or your parents! We *have* heard of Albert Einstein, Thomas Edison, Frank Zappa, and scores of others who have made names for themselves aside from the fact that they were all poor students. I'd hate to have to rely on a composition by Warren Beatty on the "Reconstruction of the South After the Civil War," or, for that matter, to have Mick Jagger conjugate some irregular verbs. When it comes to the subject of women, however, these two go to the head of the class. Any ideas of inferiority have been in your mind for a long time. Don't let them dominate your present or future thinking. What happened in the past is over. Forget it! It's not that important. Remember, an "A" in the classroom does not mean an "A" in the bedroom.

Like the "frog" man, perhaps you have to start by having something tangible to work with. OK. Make up a series of cards with phrases similar to the one Dr. Z wrote about Burt Reynolds. Some alternatives are: "He may be better in school—but when it comes to sex, *I* could teach

Albert Shanker a few things or two!"; or, "Zubin Mehta may be good with his stick in the Phil, but I'm better with mine in the filly!"; or even, "I am an unlimited faucet* and every woman is my bucket."

More creative and ambitious students may want to cut out pictures of beautiful girls and paste their pictures on the cards as well. Once this has been done, look at them each morning and night. Your subconscious will automatically become aroused and will start to say to yourself: "Look what I'm missing" or "Look what I missed last night." This will start the seed growing. Carry these cards with you before a date or an evening of barhopping. Your mind, already programmed to work for you, will pipe in, like Muzak: "Look what I'm getting tonight," or even: "The shape of things to come."

Make a list of pros and cons about yourself. Those of you who think you have nothing will be in for a big surprise. For instance, although your number one con may be: "Flop with women," think of all your pros:
1. You're alive.
2. Good health.
3. A job.**
4. You're not living in Iran.
... and so on.

All of these, coupled with the fact that you're on the road to recovery (recovering or discovering your self-confidence and integrity, that is) clearly outweigh the con(s) which can all be attributed to your feelings of inferiority (which you are going to defeat anyway) or fear of success. As Franklin Delano Roosevelt, one of our *longest* Presidents, once said, "There's nothing to fear but fear itself"—and it's a well-documented fact that he was laying plenty of pipe on the side.

---

*Not Farrah.

**Maybe not the greatest job *yet*, but you're still way ahead of others.

*What Is Integrity?*

In the last paragraph, we mentioned the word "integrity." This is probably a word you have been hearing and reading about in comic books for years. There's more to it than that. Integrity is important; in fact, it may become one of *the* most important words you'll ever learn. Having self-confidence, though a major part of the battle, does not win the war. Once you have it, you've got to *want* it. This "want" is integrity and to have integrity, one must have energy.

Hopefully, we're not going too fast here. Perhaps it would be better to give you this simple equation to remember:
INTEGRITY = ENERGY
ENERGY + SELF-CONFIDENCE = SUCCESS
You see, for true success, you need integrity or energy. Where do we get this energy from? How do we keep it constant? Once again, this is within *you*. To arouse this energy, thereby building up your integrity, we suggest the following.


*The Pavlov Method*

Pavlov was a great scientist (not to be confused with Pavlova, who was a great dancer, not to be confused with baklava, which is a Greek pastry. Confused?) Years ago, Pavlov came up with a legendary experiment called "The Reward System." This consisted of caging up dogs and not feeding them (fortunately for science, this was before the founding of the A.S.P.C.A.). Pavlov commanded these canines to perform certain functions, otherwise they wouldn't eat—food being their reward. It's amazing how many eager dogs automatically got the smarts and became conditioned to respond to their master's orders. Pavlov, who probably passed up a great career with Barnum and Bailey, stuck to his respective field, and went down in science history; of the dogs, nothing more is known.

The point we're making here is that if this can work for some Communist scientist it can probably work for you.

What are your likes—those small pleasures you enjoy so much every day? Be it eating Pop Rocks, drinking beer, lighting up a joint, whacking off, or watching Walter Cronkite—these can be your rewards.

For example, suppose you see a girl you like but you don't want to waste your time asking her out, picking her up, having dinner, seeing a show—whatever it takes to get her in bed. In other words, supposing that self-confidence has made you lazy, or, if you're still new at the self-confidence game, you're simply afraid to ask her out. Nonsense. What good is the jockey if you don't have a horse?

Program or condition yourself to be rewarded on the completion of each task—no matter how pleasing or laborious it may seem to you. To begin with, you *have* to call her up or arrange some kind of introduction. Now we agree, this can often be a drag; but until one has fully mastered HRF, one *must* go through all the bullshit. Just think if it this way: a year ago would you have even dared to speak to her? You see, HRF is working already. So you tell her that you've got two tickets to "A Chorus Line". (This show is always a good bet, although for those of you outside of the big cities, make sure that there is a production of this play running nearby before you ask. HRF may give you integrity and self-confidence, but it does nothing for stupidity.) Once the date has been arranged, treat yourself to those Pop Rocks or that joint, or the new issue of *U.S. News and World Reports*—you've earned it!

Use this reward system straight down the line. Eventually, your subconscious will become so conditioned that it will build up a resistance to laziness and/or fear. At that point, you'll no longer require rewards and will act entirely on your own.

Keeping the above in mind, you may wonder if such conditioning might not place too much exertion and pressure upon oneself? For the answer to this, turn to Step Two.

## Summary:
## Step One: Do I Like Me?

1. You must believe in *you*. Self-confidence is the first thing you must master in order to achieve psychic mind control.
2. Lack of self-confidence is frequently due to an inferiority complex. An inferiority complex is the result of some unpleasant incident from your past. Don't be dominated by your past—think only of the present and the future.
3. By listing your pros and cons, you will automatically raise your opinion of yourself. The fact that you have been unsuccessful in scoring with women is something that can be changed. Weigh this against the actuality that you're alive and in good health. Already, you're winning.
4. Merely having self-confidence is not sufficient. One has got to "want" his goal badly enough in order to attain it. This "want" is called *integrity*. Integrity will give you the necessary energy needed for your success. There are several ways to build up one's integrity. We recommend the Pavlov Method in which certain deeds, satisfying or otherwise, are compensated by rewards.

GO NO FURTHER ... unless you truly believe and wish to learn the principles of HRF.

# Step Two: PEACE = PIECE

# II

We have now established that in order for one to fully gain self-confidence, one needs integrity or energy. This energy is psychic energy, or the thinking of positive thoughts. The Pavlov or reward system helps to generate this energy, thereby releasing that almighty psychic power. Once the mind and body become conditioned and the reward system is no longer necessary, how does this power keep going? More importantly, you may ask, will I have the strength to keep it up?

Well, here's the answer: Actually, the reward system never really stops—it just changes from the tangible (physical reward objects) to the spiritual. In other words, instead of giving yourself that extra drink of coke, or even that extra snort of coke, all one will have to do is to *think* of that big 12-ounce bottle or that little 2-gram spoon. The total happiness that these objects can bring will be enough to generate that Power. This whole idea goes back to the age-old phrase: "Think pleasant thoughts." Whoever said that, whether it was Ben Franklin, Galileo, Voltaire, or someone equally silly, he *definitely* had HRF. We can therefore confidently proclaim that the one sure way to piece of ass is through peace of mind.

*How Do I Get Peace?*

This is a question that for many years plagued Cochise. He thought he could do it by signing a treaty, but, had he read his Plato, he would have known that the best way to obtain peace would have been to "clean" his soul.

Now Plato, like the late Sid Vicious, had a penchant for frequently going a bit *too* far in order to make his point. To cleanse one's soul can be a mammoth undertaking. What we want is merely to do some light spring cleaning. What we are concerned with is the mind.

*How Do I Clean My Mind?*

"Cleaning one's mind" still sounds too much like Plato. We have visions of readers pouring Lestoil into their ears. (We certainly don't want you do to that and *definitely* do not recommend it!) No, cleaning one's mind is out. *Emptying* one's mind is a far better term.

Alright, how do I empty my mind? Glad you asked. To make one's mind completely empty is easier than you may think; in fact, for most of you, it's probably downright simple. The best way to go about this is to think of your mind as a highway rest stop. At least once a day, for about fifteen minutes, "go to the bathroom" and empty or relieve yourself of all unpleasant thoughts and worries (whether they be personal, business—whatever.) Then, simply flush them away. If any worries try to come back and haunt you, be adamant and say, "Sorry, this stall is occupied." Since "emptying the mind" is a rather cumbersome expression, let us simply call this process TM, or Toilet Meditation.

As Chapter Seven (or Step Six) gives a fully-detailed breakdown of TM, allow us to continue by suggesting what one should do with one's mind, now that it is empty. Once all of your daily worries, pressures, and fears have been removed, your mind is free to think of those pleasant thoughts we were talking about earlier.

*What Kind Of Peaceful Thoughts Should I Think About?*

As an entire book can be written about this, we will generalize a bit and give you a couple of ideas.

Some people like to think of sunsets, moonlit nights, dawn in the country, green mountains, and cold blue rushing streams. That's all very beautiful, but it's also boring. Others think of words which connote "peacefulness", such as "pleasant", "lilting", "quiet", "calm", "gentle", "relaxing", and "refreshed", which is fine if you're Allen Ludden.

Our advice is not to think of peaceful thoughts as much as thinking of "pieceful" thoughts. For example, that blonde with the huge chest, whom you see every day on the bus when going to work, or the secretary in your office with the great legs, or the key to the women's dressing room on the set of "Dallas." All of these things will bring about peace of mind.

An even closer method of totally fulfulling TM is to combine the last two suggestions, or PEACE + PIECE. For example, think of some luscious females and give them peaceful nicknames, such as Serenity, Felicity, or even Satisfaction ...

One negative note here (and it's slight): the Puritans used to name their women in this manner and it's generally known what a fucked up bunch they were, prone to wearing buckles all over their bodies and putting people in stocks and such. However, as the days of Cotton Mather are past, and the only remembrance we really have of these turkeys is Thanksgiving, we wouldn't put too much stock in this.

What we do *warn* you about is not to get sidetracked in your peaceful thinking and end up pondering unpieceful thoughts! For example: "Can I satisfy that blonde?", or "I wonder if that redhead I admire is a dyke?", or even "What if Mike Curb became President?"

*When's The Best Time For TM?*

TM is ideally suited to the afternoon hours, between four and six. It is during these hours, we discovered, that the mind yearns for some kind of thoughtful relaxation. Just think about it. If you're at home during this time you usually find yourself doing nothing more stimulating than watching some banal game show, or even worse, listening to the uninspired philosophy of Fred Mertz on the umteenth rerun of *I Love Lucy*.

If you're at work, you'll have to admit that these hours are, as a rule, slump city, when the only constructive job you are doing is figuring out how much longer it is until you can leave. Why not turn this dead time into something useful? Here's your opportunity for TM. Don't *waste* your mind!

Many of you are probably thinking that meditation is some kind of sleep or nap. This is absolutely false—although a good night's sleep is closely related.

Once you have mastered TM, as well as HRF, your mind will start to work for you—long after you've physically stopped for the day. That's right, the mind works 24 hours around the clock. While you sleep, your subconscious is generating energy. To fully benefit from this, we again reiterate that you have to master and condition your mind to keep pumping out that self-confidence and integrity—even *during* slumber. This isn't as amazing as it sounds. Some people have made *entire* careers out of sleeping. Look at Robert Mitchum.

On the other hand, some people lethargically lounge around in the sun all day and mentally do absolutely nothing. These are called Californians.

Now that we've explained what this energy is and how it works, you're probably wondering: "How will I *know* it's constantly working?" (at least in the beginning), or "Can I indeed keep it up?"

This being the Case, turn to Step Three.

## Summary: Step Two: Peace = Piece

1. Once one has outgrown the reward system, one can keep that all-important Power generating by merely thinking peaceful thoughts.
2. In order to think peaceful thoughts, one must

empty one's mind. This process is known as TM, or Toilet Meditation. Meditation, or the casting out of unpeaceful thoughts, should be done at least once daily for about fifteen minutes.

3. The peaceful thoughts you think of should be combined with the "pieceful" ones—or the woman you ultimately desire. One method is to visualize the woman and to give her a peaceful nickname.

4. The best time for TM is usually between the afternoon hours of four and six. These hours, we have discovered, generally fall into the category of "slump city," when one is at his least creative.

5. When one has conditioned the mind to think peaceful/pieceful thoughts the energy will be generated on a full-time basis—even during sleep.

GO NO FURTHER ...
unless you truly
believe and wish to
learn the principles
of HRF.

# Step Three:
# MAY THE FORCE BE WITH YOU

# III

If you have been following the instructions set forth in this book so far, you should have already noticed a positive change in your attitude. Likewise, you should be feeling much better physically; better, possibly, than you have ever felt. The beginnings of an "aura" are taking root and even now the women you come into contact with should be reacting to you differently—or reacting to you *period*!

This is all due to the energy which is being generated throughout your entire system by your mind, or the "force" ... but: Can one's body constantly produce energy without breaking down? Doesn't every machine have to shut down at least occasionally? Even Rod Stewart gets tired.

We'll bet you Norman Mailer's ego that these questions are running through your mind at this very moment. *Again*, you must remember what we said at the very beginning—the one point which we designated as the absolute most important factor: YOU! If you allow yourself, or more precisely, your "mind" to get tired, it will send little messages to the various parts of your body, telling them to likewise "knock it off."

As we said in the previous chapter, meditation will clear the mind of all unpleasant thoughts. Fill the mind with peaceful thoughts and you will have a pieceful time; the body does what the mind tells it to. To complement this—again we refer to Chapter Two (our book and *not* the Neil Simon play)—a good night's sleep will leave one completely relaxed and refreshed only when the mind, which never sleeps, continues to pump out that energy.

Sleep, therefore, becomes like a battery recharger. A slight warning: even the best battery recharger will function only in relation to the type of batteries you give it. A Duracell or an Eveready will remain strong almost indefinitely. A cheapie bargain, such as the kind one gets on sale at the 5¢ & 10¢ stores, proves to us that: A) you really are not seriously interested in using the ultimate power available to you; B) you are lazily looking for a shortcut, thereby cheating yourself; or C) you refuse to take dares from Robert Conrad.

Now any of the above is a death threat; but, if you suffer from A, B, *and* C, you've *really* got a problem.

The solution to this dilemma is simple: Don't let your mind get tired. This probably sounds like an immense order but it really isn't. The only way one's mind gets tired is when it loses interest. Lack of interest causes a halt in the flow of energy. We can think of no better way to illustrate this than by recounting an actual event which occured while touring Upper Darby, a small hamlet in Pennsylvania. Pennsylvania, a state long synonymous with lack of interest, seemed like the ideal place for us to preach HRF. We weren't wrong. Our presence hadn't been known for thirty minutes when there was a knock on the door of our hotel room.

Opening the door revealed a rather well-dressed, very good-looking young man. Agreeably, his *outward* appearance seemed more than presentable; there was, however, something "inside" that seemed to scream out that all was not right. The three of us all felt this, although we could not put our fingers on just what it was until Y, using his usual sense of tact, blurted out, "Boy, this guy is *un*interesting!"

We have often chastised Y on his approach, reminding him that just because Don Rickles might approve doesn't make it right.

We ushered the lad, who was now more depressed than ever, into the center of our room. We then asked him our usual three opening questions:

"Just what is depressing you so?"

"Yes, what is the problem?"

"Yeah, what's her name?"

Upon hearing the last question, the one that always does it, the young man turned and spoke. " 'Her' name! If it was *only* "her" name! *Their* names!"

We replied that we didn't know what the hell he was talking about.

"I have a terrific problem with women!"

"We gathered that," replied Z. "What is it?"

"I'm not quite sure," came the perplexed reply, "other than ... "

"Yes!?" we all asked with anticipation.

"Well, basically, they won't leave me alone."

The three of us looked at each other strangely. This was, indeed, an unusual problem.

"Just what are you trying to pull!?" demanded X, angrily. There was just a trace of jealousy in his voice.

The man was crying now, his head in his hands. "Everywhere I go, they're all over me—like flies into shit! How can I possibly decide on the type of woman I like when they don't give me a chance to breathe. On top of that, my job has been affected. I can't concentrate on my work. What's more, they've had to take all the women out of my department. That still wasn't enough. They kept coming around: "Can you change my ribbon?" or "My blotter isn't working." Finally, they had to put me in a specially built plexiglass cage—four see-through walls. I tell you I feel like Marcel Marceau."

"Obviously," X interrupted, "they think enough of you at work to put you in a cage."

"I don't know how long *that's* going to last," screamed the pitiful man, now on the verge of hysterics. "They bribe the custodian with sex ... to let them in during lunch hour—just to watch me! I tell you it's mind-boggling—knowing that they're there ... ogling me! Some of them write their phone numbers in lipstick on my cage."

How do you leave work each day?" asked Z.

"Well, for the past three months, I've been leaving every night disguised as a Hare Krishna. It's only a matter of time, though, before they figure that one out."

"... and after work?"

"That's worse! They keep finding me in dark places, offering to buy me another drink, as if I don't know what's on their minds ..."

"Maybe you shouldn't hang out at bars?"

"Bars? What bars? That's in my apartment! They break in, sneak in, crawl in ... God, women are devious—what they won't do to get laid. On a good ... err, bad night, I throw fifty out of my bed alone!"

"Have you tried to get help?"

"It doesn't matter. They're still far too many to satisfy."

"No, no. I meant, have you been to the authorities?"

"Oh, sure. They laughed at me. Been to a psychiatrist —he threw me out! The only positive thing which has come out of this has been an offer of full-professorship at the NYU Business School! That's why, as a last resort, I thought I'd come to you. I'm desperate. I'll try anything!"

The three of us looked at each other. Certainly we couldn't deny this fellow human being help. But how? What an unusual predicament. One of us suggested that there may be such a thing as having *too much* HRF! (We decided against this as, more important than succeeding with women, HRF is supposed to provide happiness.) Eventually, we realized that there was only one solution: To teach him the fundamental principles of HRF—how to use and control it—and hope that the Power would take care of the rest. Unsure of our philosophy but desperate to try anything, the lad, armed with extensive notes, went home.

Within a week, he already seemed more secure. He was picking the women *he* wanted from out of his throngs of female admirers. The others, he threatened with violence—to himself. They reluctantly backed off. Still, even with the women *he* had picked, there remained an air of unhappiness, of boredom, if you will.

Finally, we decided (along with him) that *he simply wasn't interested in women!*

What was the next step?

We implied that he possibly was interested in men. He retaliated by socking X in the face.

How about four-legged animals?
Fruits and vegetables?
Motorized machinery?

Nope, these all drew a blank. This clown just wasn't interested in sex—period!

Then we remembered that HRF also covers other kinds of success, namely money. Hadn't this man been upset that his job was in jeopardy? It now seemed so simple. We merely changed the focus of his interests.

The result—it worked like a charm! Today, this man is incredibly successful at making money, and since making money is all that he wants to do—he is incredibly happy. He has truly taken advantage of HRF. The important thing to remember here is that: 1) there are some people who just have no interest in sex, and 2) they come from Upper Darby, PA.

In contrast, there was another man we had (figuratively) who indeed had an interest in sex, pursued it with success, and still was unhappy. There was only *one* girl crazy about him—his secretary. In fact, she was totally devoted to the jerk—but he couldn't see her for the light of day. Now, this girl wasn't exactly what you'd call beautiful; in fact, if she was yogurt she'd have been 'plain.' Naturally, this guy wanted that "really dynamite piece of ass"—chicks who frequented discos, TV models, starlets—and since he was the chairman of the board at a firm which produced superficial plastic products, he was more than qualified for exactly these types.

Never noticing this one broad who was throwing herself at him (even *we* picked up on this, as she would call us to set up his appointments), he would come to our meetings week after week, each time accompanied by a diffferent beauty, and hem and haw about how unhappy he was.

"These chicks! They're too much! You can't touch 'em here, you can't touch 'em there! 'Oh, no, don't—I bruise like a peach!' You have to screw 'em by osmosis. What's worse—when you finally do get inside them, they just lie there! They don't moan, groan, shreik, scream—nothin'. Might as well drill a hole in a brick. Makes a guy really feel like a dud, ya know. And the gloss and crap on their faces—you touch it and it's like Vincent Price in *House of Wax*.

After hearing these same complaints too many times we demanded that he give up these women and try something different. We "introduced" him to his secretary.

"Are you kidding? This *is* Vincent Price in *House of Wax*."

We reminded him that beauty was only skin deep, as well as the minor importance of outward appearance. We also told him that just because he was a business executive didn't necessarily mean that he *had* to be an asshole. This last statement wounded his ego. He took the girl home with him.

Wouldn't you know it! That was the best night of lovemaking he ever had. They've been married for six years and have seven children.

Now, what happened to this guy? Well, as we demonstrated earlier, the energy was being made all right, but it got clogged due to the fact that Mr. Businessman really didn't know what he wanted. It took, in effect, a psychic blow job, to start the energy flowing again.

Enough importance cannot be placed on avoiding getting tired, even, as we have learned, at the expense of a shift in interests. The *worst* thing that can happen is not to be interested in anything at all. People who remain in this state allow their minds to vegetate. When the mind isn't interested, the body becomes uninterested. You start to get sick, and, as frequently is the case, you die—and there is nothing more boring than a lot of dead people.


*What Is The Secret To Interest?*

The one sure key to knowing whether you are genuinely interested in something is to believe in it. If you seriously believe that you are having the best time you can possibly have, then you're interested. If your mind is interested, then your body's interested. Belief being the secret, some astute reader might observe that politicians would probably be immune to HRF. Not necessarily so. Although most of their promises and pledges are just so much of a crock, there is one thing *all* politicians *do* believe in: lying.

One senator we knew told us that he could wallow through the bullshit in his speeches by his devout belief in Faith, Hope, and Charity (Faith, Hope, and Charity were sisters who lived a convenient twenty minutes from party headquarters.)

## *How Not To Be Boring*

At this stage of the game, you should have already begun to adopt a new outlook on life. Once you have achieved self-confidence—when your mind is at peace, when the energy is flowing, when you truly believe in something—life should cease to become boring. It should be more like a game—a game where you're always the winner. This goes for your job, as well as your sex life (you may want to think of your job on Earth as *being* your sex-life, athough *never* think of your sex-life as being a job.) Do not consider any task to be work—otherwise you become trapped in the hustle and bustle of mass production. Once this has happened, you will be transformed into a human digital clock, constantly reporting miniseconds—going, going all the time, eventually breaking down. When one of these deals goes kaput, they are immediately replaced. Can *you* be replaced?

Once you have discarded the world where life consists of crossing things off a list, you'll find yourself able to devote your total existence to fun and pleasure. Let your mind do the work; *you* take it easy.

## *What's My Body Doing All This Time?*

While your mind is becoming conditioned, your body is likewise making adjustments. As far as the pursuit of women goes, there *are* some things you can do to help it along: Avoid sex between four and six in the afternoon. This is the worst time for screwing (although very good for TM). The best times are between 9:30 and 11:30 a.m. and 10:00 p.m. and 1:30 a.m.

Here's an additional helpful tip: When dining before a romantic conquest, eat light. (Salads are good.) Keep away from heavy Italian, French, and *especially* German cooking. You want to make your moves with the grace of a Fred Astaire—not Godzilla. There's nothing more embarassing than being in some chick and hearing your stomach (and various *other* parts of your anatomy) revving up like the start of the 1911 Indianapolis 500. Also, keep off Jewish food—unless you are courting your mother.

Now that your self-confidence is beginning to emerge, let's move on for some advice on *how* to use this newfound power ...

## Summary: Step Three: May The Force Be With You

1. A certain force should now be building up within you. Sleep recharges this "force" or "battery" which keeps the energy going. In order to keep this up, one must not let the mind get tired. To prevent the mind from getting tired, one must *not* lose interest, and, in order not to lose interest, one must seriously believe in his goal.
2. Life should not be thought of as a boring, day-to-day existence. One should, instead, think of life as a game—where you are always the winner. This will strengthen that aura around you.
3. While your mind is conditioning itself, your body is physically doing likewise. For your body to get the most out of a healthy sex life one should: a) avoid sex during the "slump city" hours (four to six in the afternoon), and b) if one chooses to dine before a romantic liaison, eat light.

GO NO FURTHER ...
unless you truly
believe and wish to
learn the principles
of HRF.

# Step Four: WHY NOT THE BEST?

# IV

The title of this chapter is the same as Jimmy Carter's book. He is proof alone that psychic mind control works. Jimmy was, of course, writing about himself and obviously *not* about his family. However, on the dangerous assumption that brother Billy *can* read, we suggest that he casually leaf through Jimmy's book, as it is a perfect example of what can happen if one believes.

After all, here's a guy hawking peanuts in the sticks one day, and moving into the White House the next. Now this can be attributed to many things—but *most* of all it was the direct result of Jimmy's belief. He actually *believed* that he was the best man for President of the United States—and he got it! It's a shame that he couldn't use his powers on a mass scale as, four years after his election, the United States can't believe it!

Jimmy Carter has probably learned many things while in the White House—all of which will be totally useless to him when he's back fondling his peanuts. You see, for all that Jimmy learned about life in the Big City, he forgot or "unlearned" the thing that was most important: to believe in himself.

No one will argue that Carter came on hard and strong; no one will likewise dispute the fact that he's become meeker and weaker. The reason for this is simple. Jimmy Carter thought that once he achieved his goal, that was enough. He couldn't have been further from the truth (a trait indigenous to most politicians). Once one arrives at his zenith, one must keep his mind working as hard, if not harder, in order to remain there. By arriving at one's zenith, we don't imply that you should go out and buy a new television set. What we are saying is: Once you get what you want, you have to *keep* wanting it. Keep believing in yourself.

Perhaps blame shouldn't entirely fall upon Carter. The job he opted for is a particularly strenuous and difficult one. It has been known to break even the most intelligent and competent of men. Bearing this in mind, Jimmy already had two strikes against him. The third strike, which he lost shortly after Inauguration Day, was belief. When you lose that, you lose everything. At the very least, this book should teach you not to become another Jimmy Carter. Hopefully, though, it has already done much more—most significantly, to inspire you to change your attitude; once you change your attitude, you change your life. Allow us, then, to set forth a pet theory closely adhering to the philosophies of Machiavelli, whose footsteps are far more desirable to follow than those of the bungling subject mentioned above.

### *The Mack The Knife Factor*

Niccolo Di Bernardo Machiavelli was a fifteenth-century statesman and writer. For many years he was the revered advisor to the Florentine government. Mack's theories, set forth in his classic book "The Prince" (frequently mispronounced as "Prick"), have become renowned the world over. The main staple of Nicky's philosophy was: Looking out for Numero Uno, or oneself. He preached cold, non-attachment relationships, such as: "I don't want to get involved", "Don't tell me your problems because I don't care", "You know, you really are boring" and even, occasionally, "Don't bother me or I'll splatter your brains."

One would think that such an attitude would make it difficult for Machiavelli to survive in any environment other than New York City. Wrong. Machiavelli was a great success, deeply admired and respected. Today, he is required reading in many of our high schools and colleges. Furthermore, Machiavelli has been the recipient of the highest honor Americans can bestow upon a literary genius: immortalization in Monarch Notes.

*How Can I Be Like Machiavelli?*

Machiavelli was the Fonz of his time. He always kept his cool; at best he was dispassionate. The very fact that he was disinterested enabled him to use his attitude, rather than blatantly devious means, to manipulate people. It is this same kind of thinking which will allow you to manipulate your lady. After all, isn't a Mack (a nickname derived from this genius) a pimp who selfishly uses women for his own means? Beginning to make sense, huh? And we bet you thought a Mack was just some ludicrous black guy in a Cadillac! We ask you to also remember the legendary Mack the Knife, a cold, uncaring, wonderful character from Brecht and Weill's "Threepenny Opera". True, he was no saint, but how many saints have had hit records about them sung by Bobby Darin?

A true way to Machiavellian thinking is to always expect the best things for yourself—*you* can do no wrong. In contrast, expect the worst from everyone else. This is especially easy with women. Once accomplished, your old phobia of inferiority will be replaced by one of superiority, thereby allowing you to take mental advantage of people around you.

*Changing Partners: How Machiavellian Thinking Can Help You Dump A Broad*

Once one becomes adept at HRF, he will, at some point, find himself in the uncomfortable position of having to dump some babe who doesn't want to be dumped. This is a particularly unpleasant task and it will require your full mental reserve; however, remember that the reason you are dumping her in the first place is probably because you have found someone far more intelligent, witty, and foxy.

Your new-found cold-blooded attitude will undoubtedly aid you in this situation. One can't, however, merely burst into a woman's room, break off a relationship, and tell her to go to hell—as the female's first impulse may be to kil you.

Although women, like sharks, are totally unpredictable, there are certain things to look out for. One thing *never* to do is look her directly in the eyes. Women's eyes are instant death. Poets have long compared them to limpid pools; we don't want you drowning in those pools. More importantly, eyes lie; one never knows what is going on behind them. A far more sensible alternative is to look at her hands. Keep your head at eye level to hers, but watch the hands. This is especially effective when delivering the bad news, as those great big eyes, filling up with tears, may make you feel sorry for the lady, causing you to ignore her hands, which at this moment can be reaching for that gun. Hands *never* lie.

*What If She Dumps Me?*

Instead of the dumper, you may occasionally wind up as the dumpee.

Rather than have those old feelings of inferiority return, one must prepare a full mental attack. This is where you can really fuck a woman's mind, or where true Machiavellian thinking can be used to its highest extent. You'll know something is amiss when you get a strange phone call from her, usually at some un-Godly hour of the night. This call will either begin or end or even entirely consist of the phrase, " ... we've gotta talk ... " Her voice will appear to sound weak—but cold. Already, your mind should be on guard. Never give into her by replying, "About what?" Remember, she's trying to catch you at your most helpless. That's why she called you at three in the morning in the first place. She knows that waking a sleeping person takes him by surprise and he will be less likely to be argumentative. Ha, ha! What she doesn't know is that you know HRF, and, although your body was napping, your mind *never* sleeps.

## How Can I Fuck Her Mind?

Tell her angrily that she should have known better than to call you when the Three Stooges are on. If she even *suspects* that you would place the shenanigans of Moe, Larry, and Curly (or even Shemp) above her, she'll literally go all to pieces inside. There's nothing more damaging to a woman than a blow to her ego.

If the Stooges don't play late night in your area, pick some equally idiotic show featuring banal or cartoon characters; Tom Snyder is a good choice.

If you don't have a TV set, simply tell her, "OK, anything you say, Mimsy." This phrase is guaranteed to *always* work—if, of course, the lady's name is *not* Mimsy.

If a showdown between the two of you is inevitable, so much the better. This gives you more time to prepare your strategy.

The important thing is that *wherever* you choose to meet—whether it be her office, apartment, restaurant, etc.—*never* look at her. This will immediately give you the upper hand, as, being an important meeting for her, she'll have deliberately underdressed *or* overdressed.

To drive her even *more* crazy, once she begins her difficult speech, pick up a newspaper, click your ballpoint pen loudly, and proceed to do the crossword puzzle. When she gets to the part about " ... I think it's best all around if we don't see each other anymore," interrupt her by asking if she knows a five-letter word for "prostitute".

## Machiavellian Group Therapy

Knute Rockne, the original Pat O'Brien, used to give his players "pep" talks to cheer them on to victory for Notre Dame.

To get, perhaps, an even better understanding of what Machiavellian thinking is, imagine HRF as being Knute Rockne. Your mind, once awakened to its powers, will begin to constantly deliver its *own* special kind of "pep" talks—to *you*! It is the positive power of these talks which will cheer oneself on to success, or, as Knute used to say, to enable you to: " ... get one for the Gipper ... " (perhaps, in our case, "zipper" is a better word, if you choose to be so lewd.)

Occasionally, to get these "pep" talks started, one needs a little help. This brings to mind a story told to us by "No Balls" Crowley, manager of a small town baseball league in the Midwest. "No Balls", so nicknamed by his wife—supposedly for his prowess as a pitcher—explained that one season, several years ago, his team seemed destined for last place. It didn't take Crowley long to figure out that the reason his men were striking out *on* the field was because they were striking out *off* the field.

Using his quick mental capacities, enriched by two years of Driver's Training School, "No Balls" came up with a devious plan. He withdrew his life savings and rented out an entire "cathouse". He dressed the inhabitants in simple, evening clothes and introduced them to his men as actresses from the Missouri road company of "The Trojan Women". To celebrate their arrival in town, he and his wife had decided to throw an elaborate "pre-game" party—at which both teams would attend.

"No Balls" paid the girls double to throw their "innocent" selves at his men—the key factor being that they did this in front of the opposing players. In contrast, the lassies were then paid *triple* to purposely insult the rival team, again in full display of both clubs. Crowley realized that these were dirty tricks, but then again, so were most of the girls.

Needless to say, the team's new feeling of superiority, both in themselves as well as over the other team, led them to a smashing triumph the following day. "No Balls" more than recouped his "investment", reserving for himself an everlasting place in the Machiavelli Hall of Fame.

As you can see by the above story, defeat can frequently be difficult to conquer, and may need a little push. If, however, you don't have "No Balls" around, we eagerly ask you to turn to the next chapter.

## Summary: Step Four: Why Not The Best?

1. Once one starts to believe in oneself or one's goal, he must work to keep it up or risk losing everything.
2. A good attitude to adhere to is the "Mack The Knife Factor," or Machiavellian Thinking. This consists of looking out for yourself—first and always. Using this type of thinking enables your HRF to successfully *mentally* manipulate people and will finally replace those last feelings of inferiority with superiority. This type of disinterested outlook towards others will triumphantly allow you to change your female partners at random and not become bogged down in what may result in a sticky situation. In contrast, should a woman wish to "dump" *you*, one's application of Machiavellian thinking will make your partner feel as if she has been mentally raped.

GO NO FURTHER ...
unless you fully
understand the
properties laid forth
in this chapter:

# Step Five:
# DON'T THINK OF DEFEAT— THINK OF DE BROAD

# V

The clue to this chapter is in the title. As long as you even *think* of defeat, your psychic powers will be held back. "Defeat," the thought *and* the word, *must* be castrated from your vocabulary. To better illustrate this, imagine your mind as being Dean Martin and defeat—Jerry Lewis. As long as these two are together, there will be a never-ending conflict or battle. Defeat, being totally obnoxious, will constantly try to upstage you, making you feel inferior and unable to reach your true potential. This may, in turn, drive you to drink, give you a bad reputation with peers, or even force you to do telethons. Although you may *think* that you are a success, you might as well be back in Steubenville. The only possible solution is a split, like Dean and Jerry's, for artistic differences. Once defeat has been ousted from your mind, you'll feel a new sense of freedom, security, and safety. You can now pursue your wildest and fondest dreams.

*What* Are *My Wildest And Fondest Dreams?*

They *should* be women, but, for those too long under the domination of defeat, one may have trouble remembering exactly what a woman is, let alone what to do with her.

If the above describes you, we suggest a visit to the world of fantasy. Now this doesn't mean you should or will retreat to a never-never land of make-believe. Nor does it imply that you should start looking up Ricardo

Montalban's phone number (or if your fantasies are small, Herve Villacheize's). It simply means that when the mind is given a positive idea concerning a specific wish or desire, it will do its best to start the energy flowing (in order to achieve one's goal,) depending, of course, on how deep one's convictions are.

Any person will tell you that his (or her) victories were the direct result of sincere and utter longing; their success was something that they had *dreamed* about for years.

Certainly you have fantasized about going to bed with a particular actress, or some chick at work, or even your buddy's girlfriend. Well, keep the faith, baby—set this as your goal, and if you don't get *that* woman of your dreams, we'll guarantee you'll at least get a reasonable facsimile. Bela Lugosi's last wife, many years his junior, was a hopelessly adoring fan. As a child and teenager she dreamed of meeting him and set this as her goal. She ended up *marrying* him! Now we're not saying that you'll wind up with Bela Lugosi. We merely want to point out the positive aspects of fantasizing.

The worst thing one can do is to stop in mid-fantasy and say "Who am I kidding? I don't stand a chance!" This is the type of defeat that has broken many a spirit. No matter how impossible or how bleak your prospects look —see them through. If things are at their worst, the only change possible is for the better, right? Don't give up and you'll get what you want!

*What If I Can't Fantasize?*

If you can breathe, you can fantasize. (If you can't, then of course you're dead.) Even boring people have fantasies (albeit meeting Hugh Downs or playing Pokeno doesn't exactly raise *our* blood level) but you're not a boring person, are you? You're on your way to discovering the powers of HRF. We might concede, however, that your ability to fantasize may be out of practice.

To give these abilities a little push, we suggest the purchase of several selected books and magazines, available almost everywhere, which more than colorfully illustrate what one can do with a woman. A word of warning: Although the idea of using printed matter to encourage your female fantasies may be valid, there are certain books one should *definitely* keep away from. They include "Psycho", "Helter Skelter", and "The Complete Jack The Ripper".

*If You Can Get Into It Mentally, You Can Get Into It Physically (Or Literally)*

Some people have built-in defeatist attitudes. Proof of their powers of mental thought thus becomes evident in reverse. These unfortunate folks are the failures of the world. We have all, at one time, met such persons. Prior to this book, you may have only had to look as far as your mirror. Look at it this way: if pessimistic thinking equals failure, isn't it logical that optimistic thinking will equal success?

We site the case of Judi Barton as an example. Now Judi was a very introverted person who felt that everything she became interested in was destined for failure. She was right—because she "telegraphed" her bad vibes to those around her. Studying proctology by day, Judi discovered that she had trouble making ends meet. She had to get a job.

Entertaining the thought of becoming Wild Cherry, a female punk rock star, Judi decided to get a position somehow related to the world of music. She secured an opening as salesperson for the Moby Dick Flute Company. Now Judi really didn't want to do this. "I'll make a terrible saleslady," she said. "Besides that, I don't get along with people. They'll hate me." The negative attitude quickly made her the worst of all the employees at Moby Dick. At the end of six weeks, she still hadn't sold one flute. (She even talked *herself* out of buying one!) Only two things kept Judi going: her deep desire to finally succeed at *something* and her landlady's deep devotion to finally having the rent paid. Still, Judi just couldn't throw herself into it.

By sheer luck, Judi happened to ring the doorbell of Konstantine di Medici di Nobli di Train LaZonga, the well-known madame of one of San Francisco's classiest bordellos.

"I don't suppose you'd want to buy a flute?" asked the reluctant saleslady.

The Madame gazed at her in shock. "What the hell kind of a pitch is that?"

"Well, I—don't—you see ... "

"Look, sister, I've been selling all my life and your approach is all wrong. You're a very pretty girl—there's no reason why you can't sell flutes—or anything."

"What do you mean?"

"C'mon in here and I'll show you a couple of tricks."

The rarity of being complimented started something within her; and, after six lessons from Madame LaZonga, Judi, now rid of all her defeatist inhibitions, learned the most important rule of her life: Never think of giving up. Judi took this precious advice to heart and now goes all the way everytime! She has even learned to play the musical instrument she once despised selling so—and, as a result, she has blown just about every flute in town, no matter the size, shape, or color.

Recipient of the Moby Dick Company's "Thar She Blows" Award, Judi has used the money from her unusually large "commissions" to begin her punk rock career. At this rate she reasons, soon *everyone* will equate her with Wild Cherry.

*Physical Defects*

Some people get defeatist attitudes because of the way they physically look and act. In other words, guys feel slighted because they are short, or fat, or speak with speech impediments. This is wrong. Colonel Manoogian, the great Southern plantation owner from the pre-Civil War days, spoke with a stutter. Yet, anyone could have told you that he was the most beloved and respected gentleman in all of Dixie (anyone except the Negroes, who hated Manoogian's guts and once tried to burn a cross on *his* lawn!) He was also quite something of a ladies man. How so? Simple. He never let his speech impediment get in the way of his desire to live life to the fullest. In fact, he often made fun of his own shortcomings. One memorable example of this occured in Tennessee in January of 1860 during the Chattanooga Great After-Christmas Slave Sale. The Colonel, casually conversing with his crony, Beauregard Milne, stopped to eye the next display item—a foxy young black woman named Brenda.

Brenda, whom Alex Haley would have been proud to have had as a grandmother, had all the Southern gentlemen drooling in their pants.

"Yikes!" said Beauregard to the Colonel. "Wouldn't you love to get Brenda on your plantation?'"

"I'd love to get her anywhere," replied Manoogian, "but that's a moot point."

"How do you mean, sir?" asked the surprised Mr. Milne. The Colonel, whose recent crops had been a bust, came back with his classic reply, "I can't even pronounce B-B-B-Brenda, let alone b-b-b-buy her."

Even today, the South recounts the above tale, as well as other loving anecdotes about a man whose greatness was, if anything, brought out by the fact that he had refused to give in to a physical defect. Be like the Colonel. Don't let height, speech, or any of those other trivial distractions defeat you.

## *Physical and Mental Domination*

In the last chapter, we learned how Machiavellian thinking can help you mentally dominate a person. This may have started you wondering about using physical domination, as well, or even as an alternative. Rid yourself of this thought immediately. While mental domination guarantees success, physical domination assures defeat. Physically pushing someone around is a tactic reserved only for members of the lower animal kingdom, bullies, and JAPs.

For our rural readers, a JAP (aka Jewish American Princess) is usually a second or third generation American woman whose Mommy and Daddy have catered her every whim (due to the fact that mater and pater and/or grandmater and grandpater themselves were deprived of many luxuries during their long trek here from the Old Country—almost always Poland.) She is spoiled, pampered, demanding, and generally obnoxious—having an innate urge to dominate everyone and everything she comes into contact with. JAPs are indigenous to the East Coast of the United States, particularly New York City, and especially Long Island. They have been known, however, to migrate as far west as California, and as far south as Florida, rarely bothering with any of the states in between. JAPs are formally educated either at Sarah Lawrence or Radcliff. It is here that they learn to acquire their well-renowned bad taste in clothing as well as an insatiable desire to have sex with anything in pants.

It is point number two that probably has you contemplating a relationship with a JAP, should you ever meet one. Friendly advice: DON'T! JAPs' remarkable and seemingly unrelentless sex drives, stemming from frustrated childhoods, will eventually destroy you. Unfortunately, the only way to *stop a JAP from trying to have sex with you is to marry her.*

*Marriage To A JAP*

Once the honeymoon is over, a JAP will put a ban on all sex until she is sure that everything you own has been placed in her name. This accomplished, fornication will be regulated to a "whenever-she-feels-like-it" basis. This will be almost never since the JAP will be too busy watching and scrutinizing *every* move you make ... and should you ever get out of line—may God help you.

To make matters worse, your winter vacations will be

spent in Miami, and your summers in the Catskills. Yet, this is still more desirable than staying in your own home which, due to her knack at interior decorating, has been styled in Early Disneyland.

This leaves you three alternatives: 1) divorce—which will make you a pauper for life; 2) sticking it out—which will become more unbearable every day; or 3) committing suicide—preferably hers—which will land you in jail. However, remember this! For all the unhappiness that you are going through, it doesn't even match up to the unhappiness *she* is experiencing. As we have already learned, when one uses mental domination, it achieves peace of mind; physical domination, on the other hand, is a cover for insecurity and frustration. A JAP acts domineering, because she fears that if she doesn't, everything will be taken away from her. Having been given everything in her youth, she really doesn't know *what* she wants.

*Can JAPs Be Cured?*

Yes, but it's very expensive. Like initial treatments with drug addicts, who are actually given large doses of methadone, JAPs must fight fire with fire; in other words, *money* is the ultimate cure.

Not too long ago, we were visited by one Rhoda Streisand who *demanded* our help. We gave her an appointment for three in the afternoon. Being "one of those days," we couldn't see her until 3:10. We were greeted with the following:

"What kind of people are you?! Making appointments and then not being able to keep them. Maybe *you* need help!"

We looked at each other.

"A JAP!" we said simultaneously.

"What's your problem?" asked Z.

"MY PROBLEM! *I* have no problem. It's my stupid fiancee. He's got a problem!"

"He certainly has," said Y, under his breath.

"What's his problem?" asked X.

"He doesn't like Miami Beach."

"*That's* his problem? Why is that a problem?"

"Because he loves those stupid mountains in Switzerland—Gawd, does he love those damn mountains. For that reason he doesn't want to take me to Florida for my—I mean "our" honeymoon! Isn't that the most selfish thing you've ever heard? Just because he suffers from sun poisoning ... By the way, what did you pay for that sofa?"

Again, we stared at each other. Our minds seemed to be in tune with what had to be done. It was going to be painful—but there was *no* other way. We would cure her cold turkey!, or, as we frequently call it, the "Eliot Ness Technique".

"First of all, Ms. Streisand," said X, "SHUT UP!"

She recoiled in horror, then spoke.

"You miserable ★#%!!&# Nobody *ever* talks to me like that. Furthermore, I don't have to pay you people to insult me!"

Y delivered the second, even more deadly blow. "Pay? Pay! Don't be ridiculous. ADVICE! That's what we're giving you—advice! *You* couldn't *afford* to pay us!"

She was feeling faint now and carefully sat down. "What do you mean?" she asked humbly.

At that point, our intercom buzzed. It was Z, who had left the room several minutes before.

"Yes, what is it?" asked X.

"It's Golda Meir," replied the voice of Z. "She wants to know if she can see us at 3:00 tomorrow?"

"Golda Meir?" gasped Rhoda, not believing what she was hearing.

"Absolutely not!" returned X. "3:00 is Alice Cooper's appointment."

Rhoda had started to go into a coma. "Alice Cooper—oh my Gawd!"

"Tell her we can see her Wednesday morning—before Robert Redford."

"Robert Redford? My Gawd, my Gawd!!!!"

Y turned to Rhoda. "As you can see, we're very busy

men and don't have time for your bullshit!"

"I never knew, my Gawd, my Gawd, my Gawd ..." she was now on the verge of becoming totally incoherent. X was relentless.

"Before you leave, I will give you one more bit of advice."

"What? What? Tell me ..." came the weak but desperate response.

"That dress you're wearing—don't take it to Miami Beach!"

"But I picked that dress out *myself*!"

"I know. It looks like Jackson Pollack threw up!"

All of a sudden a slight flash of strength seemed to return. "I bet you think I don't know who Jackson Pollack is, do you? Well it so happens that I just bought a print of one of his most famous paintings—and it cost $150.00!"

X trembled. We had lost her. She was an undefeatable JAP. But wait a minute. Y was sardonically grinning. Could there be a glimmer of hope? "I have the original," he said, calmly, quietly, without moving a muscle.

Rhoda Streisand collapsed on the floor. When she came to, the first thing she saw, being still on the floor, were X's shoes.

She barely managed the following: "Those ... are nice ... shoes ... What did you ... pay for ... them?"

"$2,000.00," replied X, not batting an eye.

Rhoda groaned, passed out again, and was shipped to Menninger's that very evening.

Upon her release, we proceeded to lay some HRF on her, and, ten visits later (for which, as part of the cure, we had to charge her $500.00 per) Rhoda was entirely free of her JAPness. She and Murray (her fiancee) honeymooned in Switzerland later that same year. She admits to us that she still *does* dominate her husband, but that she does it with her mind. Rhoda has become a fun, warm, loving wife, with lots of friends and oodles of happiness. She has learned that having a "strong" attitude isn't as important as having a peaceful one. Her overt personality had defeated no one but herself.

As possible as it is to cure women such as the one above, we highly recommend that you, a relative newcomer to HRF, keep away from JAPs—even it it's on a dare.

*The Name Game*

People who accept or even welcome defeat generally have bad memories. "So what?" you're saying. So this! A good memory is important—so important that it becomes an integral part of HRF. Imagine your embarassment when you can't remember the names of certain people who may be important to you. Imagine *their* embarassment if they happen to be your parents. What's more, a woman feels understandably degraded when, after a rather vigorous bedroom romp, she is still referred to as "Hey, you"!

Your memory is something that you can start to correct right now. Take out a pen and paper and begin to make a list of people you like and/or would like to be with. If you can't remember their names, do a little detective work. While probing this information, we recommend that you make additional inquiries pertaining to each individual's specific likes and dislikes.

Once your list is completed, read it aloud each night before retiring (like prayers). Pretty soon it will become a force of habit. *Everyone* loves to be remembered or recognized. This is especially true of women, who will almost certainly reciprocate by going out of their way to remember *you*.

In Chapter Four, we briefly introduced the TM factor. We now feel that you have enough information and self-confidence to further explore and fully understand this meditative process. Please turn the page and prepare to reach the highest plateau.

## Summary: Step Five: Don't Think of Defeat— Think Of De Broad

1. The word "defeat" is the most dangerous word in our vocabulary. It must be ousted from your mind. As long as there is even a slim thought of defeat, your psychic powers will be stagnated. One way to avoid defeat from entering your mind is to fantasize.
2. Anyone can fantasize. Some of us, however, may be at their low in a valley, rather than at a high on their peak. If this describes you, we suggest a little physical aid in female fantasizing. The purchase of certain magazines or books, either from your newsstand, or, more likely, via mail order, will more than start you on your way to fantasy.
3. Physical "defects," such as unusual heights, speech impediments, baldness, etc., often are the cause of defeatist attitudes. This is a wrong approach. Outward appearance is not nearly as important as inward appearance. Some of our most successful men have been victims of unusual physical defects. FDR had polio—this did not make him any less great. Leave the looks to the women. They would much rather have someone who can take good care of them than someone who is "competition."
4. Although we *do* urge Machiavellian thinking to mentally manipulate a person, never allow physical domination to become a factor of your personality. Physical domination is reserved for pushy people, bullies, and JAP's.
5. JAP's (aka Jewish American Princesses) are a certain species of women who adhere to the phrase "in name only"—theirs! They are probably the most obnoxious of the many types of female animal and can only be cured by large doses of money. One should keep away from such women at all costs.
6. To further gain the respect of your contemporaries/ adversaries, practice improving your memory, as a

bad memory is another sign of defeat. Make a list of women you know or would like to know and memorize their names, also any traits, habits, likes and/or dislikes. Everyone (especially women) loves to be recognized or remembered. Logically, they in turn will go through the trouble of remembering you.

GO NO FURTHER ...
unless you truly believe and wish to learn the principles of HRF.

# Step Six:
# WILL SHE THINK I'M A CREEP?: THE TM FACTOR

# VI

As we learned in Chapter IV, TM is the emptying of one's mind, or meditation. Now the word "meditation" itself, conjuring up images of dirty hippies and phoney gurus in the mid- and late-1960's, may leave a bad taste in some readers' minds. However, before you reach for a bottle of psychic Listerine, kindly remember that both the Beatles *and* Clint Eastwood were heavily into meditation—and we wouldn't exactly call them failures.

TM is the cure for the most dreaded malady ever to plague mankind—worry. Worry, like a cancer cut out of your body, must be evicted from your mind. Worry has caused much grief, sickness, and even death. Ulcers, high blood-pressure, coronary disorders and even the heartbreak of psoriasis have all been attributed to worry. Recently, arthritis has been added to this list—most assuredly *not* the kind of stiffening you are anticipating.

*How To Avoid Worry*

TM, or Toilet Meditation, is so named because, as you may recall from Chapter IV, we had asked you to consider your mind as being a huge toilet bowl which, at least once a day, is to be emptied of all negative thoughts. Since "worry" is a particularly easy disease to catch, and, unfortunately a difficult one to get rid of, we suggest you aid your mind along via intellectual drainage or, in fact, a mental enema.

Worry is all around us and can clog those all-too-important energy passages. By merely *refusing* to think negative thoughts you can literally force or drive all thoughts and ideas of worry and insecurity out of your mind. It will now be empty and ready to enjoy the benefits and peace (or piece) which TM can bring you.

Even with TM working for you, one may still become annoyed at the many worriers surrounding him. Resign yourself to the fact that *wherever* you go, there will always be some clown (or clowns) who will actually seem to derive pleasure in talking about fatalistic or unpleasant things, whether it be political unrest, inflation, the increasing death and murder rates, or the new CBS Fall Line-up. Avoid these people like the plague—and we mean that literally. These jokers are carriers of worry, and since murder is still officially illegal, the best you can do is to just keep away from them. When conversations begin to take on that "worry ambience" (the above topics entering the discussion) politely bow out, saying that you have to go to the bathroom. Then retreat to a quiet corner for fifteen minutes or so and, through TM, empty your mind of all you have just heard.

One young woman we know was the victim of worry. She was living with her boyfriend, an intern veterinarian who supported himself by designing T-shirts in Greenwich Village. The concentration of intelligence, combined with the pressure of striving to maintain a level of good taste, both so necessary in the T-shirt business, drove the young man to drugs. To make matters worse, he was beginning to play around with some of his women patients (the owners, of course), and his mother, an ex-WWII riveter, after visiting two weeks, stayed for six months; the old woman suffered from an acute condition and was confined to bed. Although no one could discern what kind of condition she was actually suffering from, a prescription for chicken soup and Lawrence Welk was arranged on a 24-hour, around-the-clock basis.

The young woman, whom we shall call Gloria (as that is her name), became more and more depressed, irritable, and, most of all, worried. We recommended TM and, within two weeks of exorcising the aforementioned fungus from her mind, Gloria's life changed for the better. The boyfriend, noticing how much more vibrant and refreshing *and* exciting she was, gave up the other women to devote himself to her. Now having something worth living for, he kicked the habit, passed his veterinary exam, and sold the T-shirt business at a profit. If this wasn't enough, the old mother suffered a massive coronary on Halloween, her birthday, and died. The coronary was attributed to worry, stemming from the fear that she was recovering.

Today Gloria has never been happier and will gladly tell you that TM made her elation possible.


*What Happens When The Mind Is Empty?*

Although TM can empty the mind for you, this is not sufficient. Something must take the place of all those negative thoughts. An empty mind is very eager to be occupied and unless one fills this void with something new, it will again become cluttered with negative thoughts.

What should you fill your mind with? We suggest peaceful/pieceful thoughts (see Chapter Three). Occasionally, one may wish to use physical means to start the mind thinking happy thoughts. This may consist of writing a peaceful message on an index card and carrying it with you. Our contemporaries often prescribe something to the effect of the following as a happiness-card candidate: "I feel really good when God loves me."

Well, that's very nice, but while you certainly would like to have God as a friend, we doubt you'd want him to "love" you—at least in the way we're talking about. Having God around *does* come in handy (as you'll discover in our next chapter), but right now you want five minutes on an Army cot with that blonde sitting on the third bar stool. (Judging the positive qualities of body heat, once she gets up you may want the bar stool.)

This understood, coupled with the desire to use the

index card system, we suggest something more along the lines of the following:

> The man who keeps saying,
> "Boy, I've got it made!"
> Will not be delaying
> When it's time to get laid.

*Benefits Of TM: How To Talk To Women*

We learned earlier of the advantages of memory, mainly that a good memory can help to establish relationships with the type(s) of people you really want to meet! Even more pertinent is the fact that this is an ideal method of getting women to like and appreciate you; being liked is as important for *your* ego as liking someone else is for theirs.

Once TM is combined with memory, one can store up a wide variety of stock phrases and lines to titillate women with. Basically, these conversations should consist of only two topics: you and her, in that order—or, if one prefers, the order of importance. Below are some of the more successful—albeit general—routes to follow once the initial ice has been broken.

*Clichés*

As independent as many of today's females appear to be, nothing floors them like a compliment concerning their physical attributes. Therefore, we offer the following solid bit of advice: When looking for a line, don't be afraid of clichés—women love them! Although it certainly is no crime to be clever or witty, it's no great assurance of sexual conquest either. More guys have gotten chicks into the sack with the simple phrase, "God, you're so beautiful" than all the Noel Cowards on Christopher Street.

Not too long ago, a popular TV Game show asked a

typical question which turned into an interesting experiment. The format of this show was to separate the men and women into two teams. Both teams' players, each consisting of three, were from different stations in life. The men were asked the following question: "Which would you rather have—Robert Redford's looks or Albert Einstein's brains?" The answer was unanimous: Albert Einstein's brains. Then came the women's turn. The question, slightly modified, read: "Which would you rather have, Farrah Fawcett's looks or Madame Curie's brains?" Again a unanimous response: Farrah Fawcett's looks! The facts speak for themselves.

No matter how obvious you seem to be, hit her with every cliché you've ever heard George Brent say on the Late, Late Show. Remember, it is the women who read the Harlequin romances, watch the soaps on TV, and listen to Barry Manilow. In other words, don't let idiocy or banality stand in your way. Even if *she* thinks it's corny, she'll adore you for it.

## What Next?

Women love important men. What's more, they love important *sexy* men. The positive energy now gushing forth from within you will tell her that you are indeed different and worth a closer look. But, as they say on Madison Avenue, it pays to advertise.

Spread the word around that in your circles you're a revered sex symbol. (If you've been using HRF for a while, the results will speak for themselves.) Make the woman feel that the mere fact you are speaking to her is a great honor. If you're good at this, she'll swallow everything you say (no pun intended). If you're bad, she'll probably just think you're being cute—at which point, she may say to you, "You know, you ought to be an actor." Quickly reply, "I am." Then tell her that you had a bit part in "The Godfather—Part II", but be nondescript enough so that she'll never be able to prove otherwise. After all, we wouldn't want her to find out that you really weren't in "The Godfather—Part II"—let alone had ever seen the film.

*Benefits Of TM: Silence Is Golden*

Now that you have talked about yourself—and very complimentarily, too—it's time for you to *listen* to her. Listening is one of the most important aspects of HRF. Since you want to know her (hopefully in the Biblical sense), listening is invaluable, and, it is at this point that she'll fill you in on her likes and dislikes. Again, TM can help reap the wonderful benefits a woman has to offer by showing you not only *how to listen* but what to do with the information once you have heard it.

*Listening*

When she starts to speak, use TM to empty your mind. Once this has been accomplished, start to fill it up with her thoughts—however trivial or stupid they may be. Getting one's hands on this kind of information is priceless and, for a change, will enable *you* to anticipate *her* every move! Furthermore, this mental dossier will make any female receptive to your way of thinking as she'll have at last found someone who she feels is as wonderful and intelligent as herself. In effect, you'll be fighting fire with fire as her thoughts will be coming through you. This, in turn, will provide one with the opportunity to come through her (in all probability later that evening.)

*Summing Up Listening*

Listening, like bullshitting, is an art, and there have been some great "artists" throughout history. One very rich, notable example appears nightly on NBC, and since a picture—even a TV picture—is worth a thousand words, we suggest that you watch Johnny Carson for a lesson on how to listen. In contrast, watch Merv Griffin for how *not* to. (Warning: You may literally have to watch the Carson show *every* night as Johnny frequently does not appear, working only holidays. However, Griffin, fearing he'll be replaced by Bob Barker, *always* appears.)

As stated earlier, women go ga-ga for important, sexy men. Use your HRF to come on like a well-known male your lady admires—whether it be Laurence Olivier, Clark Gable, Paul Newman, or even, depending upon her age, Erik Estrada. (Remember, however, that the statutory rape laws are probably pretty strict in your state.)

*Outward Appearances: What Should I Wear?*

Once again, we wish to stress that far too much emphasis is placed upon one's outward appearance. It is the "inside" appearance—TM working for your HRF—that counts. We will, however, suggest one or two points about dress and looks.

Outward appearance is basically an application of common sense. For instance, if you're dating a rock queen or groupie, we wouldn't advise that you dress for a White House dinner. On the other hand, when dating a debutante, don't show up looking like a member of Kiss. This simple tactic of logic is generally practiced everywhere—with the exception of Hollywood, where sartorial splendor has been banished.

One thing we *will* harp on is good hygiene. One *must* clean his outside just as one must clean his inside. Bathe (or shower, if you prefer) at least twice daily. Comb and groom your hair, trim your finger and toe nails, and, most importantly, brush your teeth. Nothing turns a girl off more than flashing a smile with Technicolor bicuspids.

*TM: A Final Point*

Think of TM as a subsidiary of HRF, a company for which you are a salesman. The product you are selling is yourself. "She" is your customer and, if the pitch is good, think of the commission you'll get!

## Summary: Step Six: Will She Think I'm A Creep: The TM Factor

1. Worry is the most infectious disease ever to plague man. It has been linked to many physical ailments, including heart attacks and arthritis. It has even caused death. Worry, like defeat, must be removed from your mind. Avoiding conversations with people who relish disaster and despair is one way but the best method is, again, through TM.
2. Once the mind has been emptied, it must be filled with positive matter. TM can help you talk to a woman by filling your now-empty mind with her thoughts. This will enable you to anticipate the woman's every move, thus intriguing and fascinating her. To pick up her thoughts, one must learn how to be a good listener.
3. Women like important, sexy men. Use your HRF to convince her that you're a revered sex symbol with many conquests to your credit. By combining TM with your memory, you can emulate the men she most admires.
4. As corny as it sounds, use TM to store up a vast thought-library of old movie clichés. No matter how "now" or "hep" a woman may be (or appear to be), a sappy compliment will floor her every time.
5. Again, outward appearance is probably the *least* important factor towards your success with women. Common sense should tell you, however, how to dress pertaining to the specific type of woman you are dating. Good hygiene, on the other hand, *is* extremely important, and, one should take pains to make sure that his outside is as clean as his inside.

GO NO FURTHER ...
unless you truly
believe and wish to
learn the principles
of HRF.

# Step Seven:
# GOD IS MY CO-PILOT

# VII

By now, if you have been following and practicing the steps in this book, there should *most definitely* be an aura surrounding you. You may ask yourself, "Where did it originate? How does the mind generate this energy I now possess? The mind is working for me, but who am I working for? WHO CONTROLS ME?" Without trying to sound like Elmer Gantry, one explanation of this power, or of any mysterious force, or of life itself, can be attributed to God.

*God As A Partner*

Certainly the name "God" itself radiates power, and, if one chooses to believe in this Supreme Being, one can *actually increase his output* by taking God on as a partner. If you have found self-confidence through HRF, imagine the unbeatable combination of you and God! What woman can possibly resist you? I mean, who's gonna stop God? This is taking the spiritual element to the ultimate limit. A woman will get much more out of copulation if she feels that she has let the Lord come into her "house." Should, per chance, a pregnancy result, think of the possibilities ...

*Does God Want Me To Be A Stud?*

You are probably asking yourself if this concept, fantastic as it sounds, makes sense. We must, as we have been doing all through this book, let the facts speak for themselves. To do this, we have to ask ourselves the following questions: (1) "Where does this Power come from?" Again, we must follow this logically right down the line, answering with another question: "Where do *we* come from?", and still another: "Where does life come from?", and so on. Eventually, as simplistic as it sounds, the only workable solution to this problem is: It has to come from somewhere. If from somewhere, why not God? Whether it be the primitive tribes on the shores of the Amazon or the primitive tribes on the shores of Palm Beach, God remains a universal idea, and, since the beginning of Creation, has been worshipped in virtually every civilization known to Man. Even business executives have been known to bow down and pray to His message, "In God We Trust," which they carry in their wallets each and every day. This is a fact. (2) Why, during the act of sex, do many women mention His name repeatedly—even if they are self-proclaimed atheists?! Explain that!

The answer to both of the above questions is simply: There is no logical explanation. Belief in God becomes apparent when one *can't* answer certain questions.

The acceptance of God in HRF may raise the following moral question: Does God approve of womanizing? While this has been argued back and forth since the Garden of Eden, we feel that we have come up with a workable answer: Yes, as long as you don't steal apples.

After all, God's foremost concern is for your happiness, and, as you have bought this book, obviously your happiness consists of a desire to go through women like Kleenex. Remember, God/the Power is *always* with you, and if you *don't* believe that—just try HRF and see what happens. Once you have a firm conviction in the first six steps, Step Seven will naturally fall into place. Doesn't it make sense that God would much rather have you screwing broads than getting your kicks whacking-off in some men's room? Of course it does.

# Summary: Step Seven: God Is My Co-Pilot

1. One should now most admittedly have an aura surrounding him. Where did this power originate? If one chooses to believe that God is responsible, and ultimately "takes" Him on as "partner," one can actually *increase* his output.
2. Every concept of God since the beginning of Creation has revolved around the idea of Him looking out for your best benefits—in order for you to reach total happiness. If the Lord has given you this Power as a means to conquer as many women as you can, He indeed must be 100% behind the idea.

Now that you have read the Seven Steps to Psychic Mind Control—go out and have some fun. We don't have to wish you luck—just congratulations.

One additional note: for 100% black-and-white proof of Psychic Mind Control, turn to the next and last chapter. It consists of the results of 15 of the many HRF graduates. Read what they have to say and prepare to join them in their success.

Once again, congratulations ...

# RABID RESULTS

*The following fifteen people have mastered or have known someone who has achieved HRF.*

# Part One: "GUYS ..."

1) **Name:** George Bailey
   **Address:** Bedford Falls, New York
   **Occupation:** President, Bailey Building & Loan Company

"I've always had two dreams: to get any girl I wanted, and to produce a Broadway show ... When I first heard about this mind control stuff, I have to admit that I was skeptical—but, being in the loan business, I realized that sometimes you've got to take a chance. So, I approached this as I would a prospective business deal and tried it. *I still can't believe the results!* Not only am I getting plenty of interest, but the term "lay-away plan" has taken on a whole new meaning! Women are actually *putty* in my hands—and there's no mess afterwards. Equally amazing is the fact that my original idea for a Broadway show, "Archiemania"—a view of the turbulent '60's as seen through the music of my favorite rock group—is finally getting underway. Of course, Bedford Falls isn't exactly Broadway but I bet even Shakespeare had to open out of town. My philosophy now is: 'It's a wonderful life'—and man, you just watch my smoke!"

2) **Name:** Silas Kane
   **Address:** St. Croix, Virgin Islands
   **Occupation:** Professional photographer

"Since the time I reached puberty, I've desired women —and that's about it! Desired them—and nothing else!

My glamorous occupation as a professional photographer put me into close contact with many a foxy chick—but after the first date (where I wouldn't get anyplace anyway) they dumped me. They didn't want to have anything to do with me. This was a real blow to my masculinity and I sought psychiatric help. My doctor attributed my failure with women to my obsession with the Three Stooges, particularly Moe Howard.

"As a child, the Stooges were my favorites and I would often dream of meeting them in person. As you know, a lot of people try to emulate their favorite movie stars—I was no exception. I wanted to be Moe!

"As a result of this phobia, whenever I would date these beautiful models, I'd attempt to gouge their eyes out, rip the hair from their scalps (as Moe frequently did to Larry), and generally slap them around. The only reward I was getting from my toils was frustration. As soon as I'd poke their eyes out or try to burn them with a hot iron, or something like that—they'd run out like a shot (the ones who still had use of their legs; the others would just scream). I couldn't understand it. *I* was having fun; I figured that women just didn't know how to have a good time.

"Finally, out of desperation (and man, was I desperate), I tried these Seven Steps and the change that occurred was like night and day. I have a power now I never knew I had. Now, women actually *beg me* to knock them around. In fact, I've discovered that there are *specific types* of broads who crave the same kind of excitement I do—they even have their own clothes to wear. Right now, I'm seeing this babe from New Jersey and she is fulfilling every one of my *wildest dreams*. This chick is one *mean* love machine. When she lets loose, no part of your body is safe. And to think, if it wasn't for HRF, I'd still be upset with those dopey models. (Now, some of them come to *me*. I spit in their faces.) Moe would be proud."

*George Bailey*

*Silas Kane*

*Dwight Frye*

3) Name: Dwight Frye
   Address: Carmel, California
   Occupation: Exterminator

"As you can see by my occupation, I'm an exterminator. We're usually not too exciting a lot—but we have the same fantasies *you* do. HRF has been able to help me act out some of these fantasies. I now "get lucky" *whenever* I hit a singles joint. The fun really begins when I do house calls on single women, or, women whose husbands are at work; I mean I can barely wait to start spraying. I can't get over it: WOMEN—hundreds of them, thousands of them, millions of them—and with only *one* thing on their minds: ME! That's what I learned from HRF."


4) Name: Fernando P. Coglione
   Address: Ozone Park, Queens (NYC)
   Occupation: Sausage Maker

"Ever since the doctor slapped me, I've been hot for broads. To make matters worse, I'm Italian. This combination makes my sex drive—is that what you call it?—a contender for the Indianapolis 500.
"I was *always* getting lots of women—don't get me wrong—but I just wasn't "satisfied," you know what I mean? I had a real problem. Here I was, thirty-five years old, living in Queens, and working in the meat business— Hey, wait a minute! don't get me wrong again! I'm not "Marty," you know, Ernest Borgnine! Like I said, I was getting plenty, everything I want going for me, but my Neopolitan appetite just wasn't being filled. For an Italian, this is the worst that can happen, almost as bad as paying your income tax. Naturally, I was worried; I started to read up —you know, medical books. I thought I maybe I was having a change of life or something. Anyhow, after a lot of reading and asking around, someone put me onto HRF —and baby, that did it! I discovered that what I was getting was not what I really

wanted; these women weren't really the types I desired. To put it in other words, as we say in the trade: "Too much white meat is boring."

"That's exactly what I was getting: white meat—loads of Catholic white meat—and what I really wanted was schmorgasbord!

"I wanted black women and Puerto Rican women. Fortunately, living in New York gave me access to large quantities of both. I wanted Orientals, Indians, dwarfs, anything! It was like a cell block being opened in my head. HRF taught me how to make myself happy and gave me the powers to do it. And, since I've discovered body paint, I can even tolerate white women again. Paisan, I've learned how to live!"


5) **Name: Elliot Sternwallow**
   **Address: Climax, Michigan**
   **Occupation: Avant-garde musician**

"Musicians, as a rule, never have trouble with women. For years, I'd get many a bitch in the sack by telling them I was Dave Brubeck. Women are such star-fuckers. The only problem was that I didn't want to be Dave Brubeck —I wanted to be *me*—and I wanted *women to want me*. Scoring with broads became an unpleasant chore—you know, like going to the dentist: You knew you were going to get drilled, but it hurt inside.

"I was also getting sick of the types of chippies we avant-garde musicians would always meet: esoteric, phoney stiffs—talking about suicide and Proust (I mean *common*: Greenwich Village, 1957!)—or those groupies: horny, hot bitches yearning for a fast fuck. I mean, you get pretty sick of the same shit every friggin' day! To top that off, my playing was beginning to suffer—like it *too* wasn't sure who *I* really was ...

*Fernando P. Coglione*

*Elliot Sternwallow*

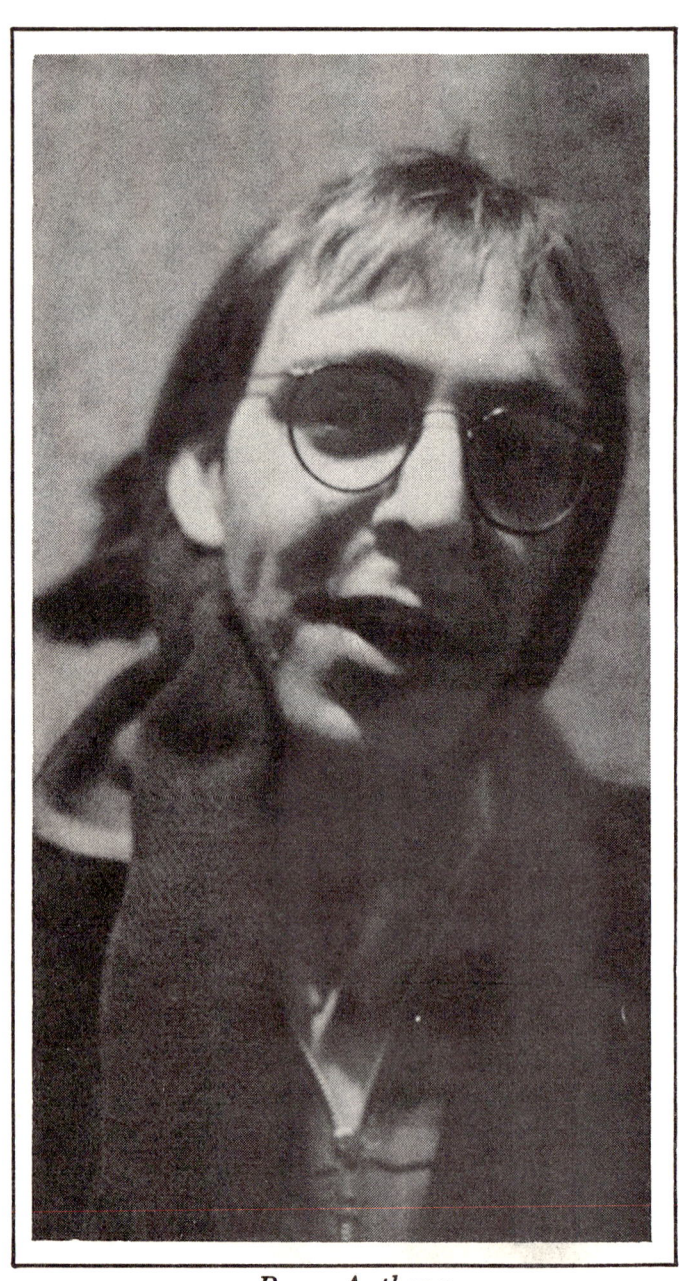
*Bruno Anthony*

"Then a buddy told me about HRF, and like WOW—my entire mental outlook changed.

"Now, these groupies go for *me*—but the Hell with them. There are other types of women in this world: artists, writers, waitresses (most of whom *are* artists and writers), UFT workers ... the list is endless. I'm just mad at myself for living in a shell *this* long. There's so much out there and it's all mine. My music has *really* improved: even *I* don't know what I'm playing!

HRF is fab, baby! I've tried a lot of these self-help things and yours is the best. I hope the whole movement really takes off for you. Then, you can open some kind of an institution. I could fill it with my friends alone—in fact, my whole union! Keep up the good work!"


6) **Bruno Antony**
   **Address: Washington, D.C.**
   **Occupation: Advertising executive**

"My dad was a big football player, figuratively speaking. He never could understand why I had no girl friends. I was afraid to admit to him or to my friends that I just didn't like women. I always hung out with a lot of pretty girls, but they were just some of the boys, don't you know.

"This fear of shaming my parents and losing my friends prevented me from seeing men my own age. Either way, I wasn't getting anything!

HRF changed all that for me; I learned to conquer all my fears. I am living *my* life and *not* my parents'—no matter how big my father is. As for my friends, if they don't approve of my preferences, then they're not the true-blue companions I thought them to be in the first place ...

I am now living life to the fullest.

May I just say, God bless you people who developed the HRF plan. If it hadn't been for you, I'd have never met Guy on that train ..."

7) **Name: Webbo Fordyce**
   **Address: New York, NY**
   **Occupation: Bank clerk**

"I tried every one of those "pick-up girls" books and magazines. All they did was to get me excited ... Then I went to this psychic mind control meeting. I didn't really know what it was—I thought I could maybe pick up some girls (but there were just guys there; shit, I was hard-up!). What I *did* pick up was a new life, man. I used to think that every chick I saw and liked thought, 'Oh wow—here comes that Webbo trying to hit me for a quick lay. Whatta jerk!' Now I think, 'Hey, I bet these horny women are hurting for my cock!"—and they are! I never connected the mind with humping—but now, sweetheart, you can call me Mr. Positive Thinker!"

8) **Name: Jett Rink**
   **Address: Provo, Utah**
   **Occupation: Rancher and ballet instructor**

"Ranchin' and dancin' are my bread and butter, and, while I've made a lot of bread at both, I have to admit that I wasn't getting too much butter—if ya know what I mean ...

I couldn't tell those sweet, young pirouetting things I taught (who I was and am absolutely horny about) that I spent the rest of my time with cows. To put the shoe on the other foot, I couldn't tell my fellow cowboys that I was teaching ballet. They think that's sissy stuff.

I became afraid of my students *and* my co-workers. I became ornery and insecure. The mind control folks straightened me out, though. Buddy, *believe me* when I say that I could actually *feel* that 'power.' HRF gave me enough courage to ask one of my lovelies out for a ride through the ranch. She jumped at the chance, bein' she *really* got off on horses! Can you imagine that?! ... And watching her get all excited riding bareback on some sweaty animal got *me* all excited! Well sir, the only

*Webbo Fordyce*

*Jett Rink*

*Julio Cortez*

sweaty animal she rides now is me—but brother, that doesn't stop the rest of my class ...

As far as my co-workers are concerned, they all got so danged jealous and horny that they're asking me to teach *them* dancin'. To think, I was afraid of women; to think, I was afraid of what my friends thought of my dancing ... Now I'm as proud of what I do as *who* I do. May the Lord be with you HRF people ..."

### 9) Name: Julio Cortez
   Address: Cincinnatti, Ohio
   Occupation: Gardener

"As you can see by the above, I am a gardener by profession. I know flowers. What I *didn't* know was women. I found out early that fucking can get you fucked up! ... I'd see a girl I liked and get all excited ... I'd start to sweat and stammer; I was a real jerk. Naturally, they'd reject me. So what did I do? The only thing I knew how—I'd retreat into the world of flora and fauna. In plants, with their cool, refreshing beauty, I found peace—the peace of nature. When I told this to a friend of mine (who, by the way does not wish to be identified, and is *not* a plant), he told me that I could apply my method for peace to HRF, or the Seven Steps to Psychic Mind Control.

"I wasn't sure if he was kidding or not but I decided to take a chance; I'm glad I did. By mastering these seven steps, particularly TM, I have learned to be *constantly* at peace with myself—wherever I am or whoever I'm in ... I filled my mind with the women I desired and then gave them the nicknames of the flowers I so loved: Rose, Daisy, Sumac ...

"No more getting sweaty and clumsy around females; on the contrary, my coolness and the obvious love which I now have for women/flowers becomes magically displayed, and attracts *them* to me! ...

For me, sex has become as pleasant a reward as a jaunt in the garden. I am no longer a jerk with women. In fact, I could pluck them all day."

*Marnie Edgar*

# Part Two:
# " ... AND DOLLS"

1) **Name: Marnie Edgar**
   **Address: Boston, Massachusetts**
   **Occupation: Free-lance writer**

"I don't believe in miracles—at least I didn't until I came across HRF. I was really fucked up. Although I desired men, I also hated them, especially when they would try to touch me—Then I would see red! I went to a psychiatrist. He told me that my hatred of men was really a fear of the male gender and of sex itself. Furthermore, he explained that this fear bred insecurity and was probably responsible for my chronic lying. He concluded that this was all the result of some unpleasant incident in my youth. That was fine, Doc, but meanwhile, I'd become so damned horny that I was constantly fingering myself, often in public (always in private).

"Although it was against his ethics, my psychiatrist—that wonderful man—told me about HRF, which he had heard about at a party. I quickly devoted myself to this system and now I'm totally cured. As a play on word conjugations (which we free lance writers must have a complete knowledge of): I don't lie anymore, but I get laid on the average of three to four times a week—and my average is improving.

Thank you, HRF, for making me a complete woman ... And that's the truth!"

2) **Name: Charlotte Innwood**
   **Address: Plainfield, N.J.**
   **Occupation: Department store buyer**

"You guys are really wearing me out!

"Being a department store buyer, I'm constantly thrown into contact with a lot of men. Now I was never one to be modest, especially about myself. Let's face it: I'm a pretty foxy chick and nothing gives me more pleasure than a good fuck. If a guy starts to come on to me, and he's got his shit pretty much together—that's it: he's got himself a 5'5" box of caged heat for the night ...

"So, all of a sudden, I'm really freaking out because every guy at work starts coming on like Errol Flynn— and I *can't* turn the lovable bastards down. I really can't! I mean, lately, if I had as many pricks sticking out of me as I have sticking *into* me, I'd be a fucking porcupine ...

"Then I find out that they're all hooked on this psychic mind control stuff. At first I laughed, but now I'm starting to get sore (Literally, honey). I mean, a woman can only screw so much! ... I've gotta start learning this HRF stuff myself."


3) **Name: Joy Butterfield**
   **Address: Laramie, Wyoming**
   **Occupation: Waitress**

"I've been waitressing for about five years so believe me I've heard every line you can think of—or so I thought.

"One day, last summer, this fella comes over to my station. I ask what he wants and he says nothing—he just wants to look at me. Ordinarily, I'd call the manager but there was *something* about this man: he wasn't really terrific or macho ... but he was *different*.

"Finally, after about three hours (we were getting ready to close), I asked him again if he wanted any food. He looked up at me and smiled; he asked me my name. I

*Charlotte Innwood*

*Joy Butterfield*

*Lizabeth Scott*

said it was "Joy." He replied, "Joy, I'd love to undress you and smear your body with one of these ketchup dispensers. You'd make a lovely hamburger and I'd like to do you right over this table."

"Wow! I freaked! I'd *never* heard that one before ... This guy was just *so sure* of himself ... I found myself asking to lock up ... and then we did it—all alone in the restaurant—ketchup and everything. I'd served the Blue Plate Special many times but I'd never been one! ... He told me that he had been watching me for months but it wasn't until HRF that he felt the time was right to come in and make his moves. I was so glad he did. Having been through several of these self-help programs myself, and, as he was now sensuously massaging whipped cream all over me (it was time for dessert), I came to the following conclusion: this was *definitely* better than E.S.T.

"After he personally cleaned me off, he rubbed my entire body with what he called my namesake, you know, that liquid soap. He said he wanted to "see himself." So did I: *in me*—every night!

"Now that this book is being written, I want to learn HRF for myself ... For those millions who undoubtedly will read it, may I just say: Bon appetit!"


4) **Name: Lizabeth Scott**
   **Address: Taos, New Mexico**
   **Occupation: Hooker**

"I've been turning tricks down here for years, since I was thirteen. I used to think I knew what men wanted, but now I'm not so sure. Lately, they've been teaching *me* a few tricks.

"For me, being a whore is just like being a secretary: it's just a job. I don't particularly get any kicks from fucking johns—just money. It's a business. The problem is that now this client I know, a fireman, is beginning to make me feel kinda funny while we're doing it—and I start to enjoy it! Good girls *don't* but I *do!* What's worse, I start to forfeit my fees. (In fact, *I even gave* Smokey the Bear some bread!) But I can't help myself: he's *soooooo* good ... As great as he is at his job, I know that when he sticks his hose into me, he'll *never* put out *my* fire. I asked him his secret; he laughs at me and says, "HRF, kitten."

"I found out that you guys are behind this group, or whatever it is. I figure for making me feel "whole"—you know what I mean—I owe you all thanks. At the same time I wanna kick ya's in the balls: I'm going bankrupt! To add insult to injury, wherever we go, we're known as hooker and ladder ...


5) **Name: Nina Tobias**
   **Address: Hollywood, California**
   **Occupation: Sunset Strip Drug Administrator**

"Hey, like WOW, this stuff is amazing! ... I bet if it was a drug, *all* of my junkies and acid heads would be strung out on it, you know ...

"There was this one guy who was *really* gone—I mean he made me sick, you know? When you can't control what you're doing, I don't like it! ...

"Anyway, he used your system to kick his habit. Then he starts to come around to ask me out. Me! His social worker. I COULDN'T BELIEVE IT! I mean he used to be a scrunge bucket with legs ... but he's not now because he's off the junk and on top of me. You guessed right. I accepted. I don't know why really—except that I wanted to, or maybe even I *had* to. Does that sound perverse? All we do now is ride around on his cycle, raise Hell, and have *funnnnnnnn*!

"I used to think that he was very lucky having someone like me for a social worker. Now I feel lucky for having him ...

"He wants me to go with him to Rome to make movies and do a lot of things, you know ... My answer is: 'Man, I'll go anywhere because I want MORE!'"

*Nina Tobias*

6) Name: Nancy Gollum
   Address: Nome, Alaska
   Occupation: Architectural designer

The following conversation took place over the telephone between myself (X) and Nancy Gollum on May 3, 1979:*

X: Hello?

Nancy Gollum: Hello. Are you the HFR people?

X: HRF. Yes, can we help you?

Nancy: I have a terrible problem ...

X: What is the nature of this "problem"?

Nancy: Well, as you can discern from my voice, I am a woman ...

X: Yes.

Nancy: I am also ... gay ...

X: Oh?

Nancy: ... and black.

X: Don't you think you're overdoing it?

Nancy: You see ... I ...

X: Look, Miss ...

Nancy: Gollum. Nancy Gollum.

X: Miss Gollum. I take it your problem involves your gender, color, and sexual preference. Is that right?

Nancy: That's exactly right!

X: Before this conversation begins to take on the characteristics of "I've Got A Secret," why don't you just tell us *how* these 'things' pose a problem.

Nancy: Well, today it seems that companies like to be "first" in hiring certain types. It's

---

*We tape *all* of our conversations.—X, Y, and Z.

apparently quite a feather in their caps. They bend over backwards to be able to say that they have a woman, a black, or a gay person on their staff. I'm all *three*! I don't know if I'm coming or going ...

**X:** Do I detect the sound of tears?

**Nancy:** That's exactly right.

**X:** Just what do you do for a living?

**Nancy:** I'm an architectural designer.

**X:** I see. Work here?

**Nancy:** Nome, Alaska.

**X:** You're not calling collect, are you?

**Nancy:** No, a bunch of us are down for a convention.

**X:** Okay. Go on.

**Nancy:** Well, my problem mainly consists of my own insecurity. Was I hired because of the *things* I am, or because of *what* I am?

**X:** The "what" being an architectural designer ...

**Nancy:** That's exactly right.

**X:** Well, there seems to be little that we can do for you over the phone ...

**Nancy:** I'm a *damned good* architectural designer too! Unfortunately, as a result of all this, my love life has been really screwed up. I get all these phoney baloney "trendy" lovers.

**X:** Because you're an architectural designer???

**Nancy:** NO! ... Because I'm ... hmmmm ... you know ...

**X:** Oh. Well, as I was saying, there's little we can do for you over the phone. Why don't you drop by and we'll give you some leaflets and basics on HRF.

**Nancy:** You mean come by to your place?
**X:** That's exactly right.

Nancy, the insecure black, gay, woman executive, *did* drop by our office, and, several weeks later, we received the following letter from Nome:

> Dear Guys:
>
> I hope you have all the success with HRF that I have had ... I now know that I am *me*—and that's the best there is ... My new self-confidence has made me a stronger person. This has obviously been evident in my work as I have been promoted to Head Architectural Designer of my company—with a *very* nice raise to boot!
>
> As for my love life, I've met some truly wonderful women who are, for a change, straight in every way—except one, of course.
>
> Best Wishes,
> Nancy
>
> P.S. I think that your idea to do a book on HRF is terrific\*. I am enclosing a photo of me, which you are certainly welcome to use as a case history should the book happen.

---

\*We had discussed the prospect of a book during Ms. Gollum's visit with us.—X, Y, and Z

*Nancy Gollum*